Sew Me Wide-Eyed to the Fabric of Your Tongue

Poems for the 21st century

Dennis Collins Johnson

Copyright © 2020 by Dennis Collins Johnson. All rights reserved.

ISBN: 978-1-938394-58-4

Library of Congress Control Number: 2020923937

published by:
Great Life Press
Rye New Hampshire USA 03870

www.greatlifepress.com

Book design and art: Grace Peirce

*For Grace,
who proved to me that life
can save the best until last.*

Saints have no moderation, nor do poets, just exuberance.
—Anne Sexton

Contents

A Rainy New Hampshire Night	1
A Short Treatment	2
American Gov.	3
Am I Still	5
Apocalypse	6
Arizona	7
Beasts	8
Bells	9
Better Best Of	10
Birthday	11
Blues for Her	15
Camp	17
Campaign	18
Chairs	19
Chide Not	20
Christmas Together	21
Conflict	22
Cords	24
Creamery	28
Creature	31
Cry3	32
Dear Silly and Quirky	33
Dippledy Doodledy	35
Don't Do It	36
Dr. Livingstone, I Presume	37
Dreams	38
Duke	39
Explorers	41
Fall Was Never So	42
Fifty	43
Final Score	44
Foolishness	47
Four Wheels and a Desert Flower	48
Fridays	50
Gas Station Restroom	51
Gaslight	53

Gone	54
Good Kills	55
Harbor	56
Help	57
In the Madness	58
January Road	60
Joking	61
Lafayette's Bed	62
Lament for My Father	63
Last Valentine	64
Listen	65
Little Yellow Football	66
Midnight	67
New Blue Shoes	68
No Towel Is Safe	69
Nor'easter	70
Oh No	71
Out of State Plates	72
Party	75
Pears	76
Portrait of the Lady and the Rhinoceros	78
Proof	79
Pruning	80
Questions	81
Ragged Boy	83
Remnants	84
Ride	85
Rivers	86
Rose-Quilted Beds	88
Rules for Life	90
Sarah Radiant	95
Second Skin	96
Session	97
Shootout	98
Snowing	100
So I'm Coming Around a Corner	101
Song for the Children	103
Sonnet Odyssey	104

Spooncatcher	105
Startled	106
Stieglitz You and I	108
Stuffed Animal Crisis	109
Stupid Poem	110
Submission	111
Synchronicity	113
Tears for Luke	114
Test	116
The Assembly	118
The Ballerina and the Clown	119
The Chickadee	121
The Day He Quit	123
The Gallery	125
The Great Canola Oil Controversy	126
The Ground Eaters	129
The Kid Plays Hearts	130
The Kiss	131
The Last Bale	135
The Last Days of PomPom	136
The Liberation	137
The Massage	138
The Orchard	140
The Tarriance	141
Thoughts	142
Thoughts on a cool summers eve in April	143
To a Former Valentine	144
Two Valentine Limericks	145
Undazzled	146
Unfortunato's Lament	147
Visually Arresting	148
Watching Her Sleep	150
Were the Woman I	151
What if doctors traded places with carnival barkers?	152
What the President Didn't Say	153
Witsa	155

A Rainy New Hampshire Night

A rainy New Hampshire night
wind stormed into my kitchen as I
passed an open window, and it
sideswiped my sky-gray hair,
and took me by the shoulders and
shook me, and whistled Lennon
on the bus stop bench inside my mind.
I could feel the ocean of it
and hear the gulls' children laugh. Then
from somewhere over smoothing rocks,
a gust of life swept through me,
and it whispered in my ear,
and it whispered
your name.

A Short Treatment

This poem is for you. Plain,
it is meant to compliment
your beauty. Simple, it is
meant to recall your
complexity. Short, it is meant
to represent the infinity of
my affection. Without meter
or rhyme, it gives
all, asks nothing.

American Gov

Fat white guys
in slick suits and neckties
telling us we have
to cut back on everything.
Except the killing. That's right,
the old, the young, the hurting,
the helpless, the retired, the
working, the looking for work,
the can't work, the middle class,
the lower class, the no class,
the innocent, the disturbed, the
families, the couples, the lonelies.
Have to cut back. Have to
cut back on everything.
Except the upper class.
Except the killing. They
want us to give them more
for that, obviously because
there has not been sufficient
killing, not killing enough to
satisfy their profit margin,
and their bottom line,
and their security concerns,
and their national interest,
and their corporate mission.
And their corporate
missionaries preach
fat white guys gospel,
and they make it sing,
and it sings of sense to many of us:
go ahead, cut us back if
that's what it takes to
do the job, be safe, get ahead,
beat the odds, enjoy life,
play the game, and stand up
to evil. Cut us

back. Except the killing.
We'll trust you to know how
many killings is enough and
when we need more. And
please, send our children out
to the killing
so they may learn how sacrifice
keeps us free,
as we must be. And afterwards,
if they return,
they can hold their medals
to their shrapneled bodies
with their
amputated arms and console themselves
on bitter nights
with the pieces of a woman
and the children of death
that sleep with them always.

Am I Still

Am I still an actor
When I'm no longer acting
Am I still a dancer
If I no longer can dance

Am I still a person
When I'm no longer in person
Am I still a chance taker
If I no longer take chance

Will I still be thoughtful
When I'm no longer thinking
Will I still see clearly
When I clearly can't see

Won't time seem like butter
On the bread of the morning
Won't love seem like lashes
On the eye of the sea

Apocalypse

An armed sunset mobilized
across Amish heavens, halted
me deep in thoughts of you beside
an obliterated cornfield, and
gave me sole command of the final
phalanxes of golds and pinks as they
advanced bravely over
tiny farmhouses.

The campaign was brief. Merciless
gray battalions charged
relentlessly, routing my vanquished
rebel skies until their
faded colors fell fluttering, and
paled, they withdrew before the
invading night.

Passing cars winked acknowledgment
of my cornfield conscription,
veering around me, but never
stopping to ally themselves, or
attempting to wrest from
me my star-crossed command.

Alone
in the aftermath, no
Amish guard having appeared to
escort me from the moonless
battlefield, I watched while the
earth executed the sun, and twilight
officers posted celestial sentries, before I
finally retreated to my
car and surrendered once
more to thoughts
of you.

Arizona

Flagstaff in the fall.
Fifteen dollars a day
for this trailer, this tiny
immobile home, squeezing sideways
to pass in the hall. You in my blue shirt,
with girl eyes to match. Mountain
autumn nights exploring you,
exploring me.
The photographs a geographic
of our woodside voyages to the
seven golden cities of the seven
deadly sins — Seven Brides choreography
bashful Broadway never saw. Then
losing you
to the bright gloom, treed
by the beast, by the horned beast,
by the beautied beast.
Incongruous along the road,
white dress with white hot anger to match
in the hunting headlights.
Arizona! Arizona,
what desert drank us? What
blinding sea blew us?
What cradled craft crawled us here in a nursery night?
My belt loops in her fingers, praying,
pulling, tugging, crying "Won't let go! No, can't let go!
Stay with me! Please don't go!"
It's been centuries since I undid her holy hands
their knotted grasp.
The belt loops now are
someone else's dust.
Her tears were
stronger gripped.

Beasts

She whispered llama
words, but lions crouched
to leap from her eyes.

Now that finally she is
gone, exuberant silence
licks my ears with
a retriever's tongue,
and rubs its cold
nose on my solitude.

And my heart falls as heavily
as brass feathers wrenched
from flagstaff eagles.

Bells

I'm trying to write a poem
for you, but strangely
enough E. A. Poe's
The Bells keeps running
through my head, even
though I try to
concentrate on you,
hear the which isn't
at all *to the tintinnabulation*
difficult because I do
find you *mellow wedding
bells, golden bells* easy
to think about. But the
darn *how they scream
out their affright* poem
just won't go away.
So I tried a little wine
to see if a *leaping higher
higher higher with a
desperate* glass will
relax me. But to no avail.
So *from the rust within
their throats there is a
groan* I'll write you a
poem another *of the
bells* time. I hope you
*bells bells bells bells
bells bells* understand.

Better Best Of

Gene,
you are
truly my brother.
Even though we
don't share the
same mother,
it's as if it's true.
And even though
we don't share
the same father,
in a way we do.
And although I
love my woman
very much, when
it comes to how best
best of friends can be,
there ain't no
better best of
than you and me

Birthday

I

So you're four today, huh? You're getting so big. And such a handsome fellow too!

Smiles

As soon as I finish doing the frosting here, you and your sister and I will have a piece or two, or maybe we'll eat the whole thing!

Laughs

I'll tell you one thing, this sure is a pretty day for a birthday. I hope the sky is as blue on my birthday.

Blue sunlight

Here, you give this to your sister and then you can have the biggest piece. And I'll have all the rest.

Dismay

Nah, I wouldn't do that, my man.

Knock

Yeah, Ned, what is it?

Pills

What pills?

Jay

Goddamn it, it's my son's birthday today! Why don't the both of you just take a gun and put yourselves out of your misery?

Everybody says that

You stay here, son. Come on.

Angry walk

Jay, did you take all of these? Did you drink this? Was it full when he started? How about the pills?

Full

Damn it Jay, I can't let you die. I'd like to, but I just can't.

You got no phone, right? I'll go call an ambulance.

Walk slow

A man on my road just tried to kill himself with a bunch of pills and some vodka. You'd better come get him.

Siren and blue lights

These are what he took, plus all that vodka.

Stretcher

Another thirty minutes would have been too late, huh? Stupid.

Thanks

He looks up at me from the stretcher and says thanks. Was that really thanks or just sarcasm?

Back

Couldn't let him die on your birthday. Make him do it some other day. On somebody else's birthday.

Blue sunlight

II

Hello Jay. Come on in, oh, and your lady. What are you doing back up here in the mountains? Exactly a year since I last saw you.

Visit

So you're clean now, huh? Great, glad to hear it!

Kids

Oh, they're out back playing in the garden. She thought he got bit by a scorpion. They did find one, but he seems to be fine. Couldn't find a bite. It's his birthday.

Ned

I guess he's up at his place. They took his license away, so he doesn't go out much. Maybe once a month he comes over and asks me for a ride. His relatives never come to visit. Nobody comes to visit.

Leaving

Thanks for coming by, Jay. See you again.

Reappearance

Are you sure he's dead?

Head

Why don't you stay here and wait for the police?

Shaking

Now maybe his relatives will come.

Three weeks later

I wish they hadn't left his porchlight on. It's like he's still there. Except for the quiet. I remember him once after he was in an institution for nine days. Straight for nine days. When he got out he was the most lucid and gentle man... but two days later drunk and incoherent again. Cut and bruised continually from constant falls. Dazed. Then, hitting his head on that table corner as he fell...

One month later

I really wish they hadn't left his porchlight on. Ned, I hope you do better in the next world.

Everybody says that

Blues for Her

Cross-legged on the floor,
she listened as I played.
She smiled and blushed and
cast dark eyes down, and then looked
up again from behind
gently lethal lashes, knowing
somehow the song was blues for her, though I
hadn't written it for her, but I
could have had I known her then.
I finished the song and asked
her to play. "I can't,"
she said sadly. So
I showed her a blues scale,
and brought her dusty guitar out
from behind the sofa for the sake
of the blues woman she wanted to be.
She showed me the tape she had
bought full of obscure blues players, good
but obscure, like a chromed pawn shop guitar.
Then we played, me on rhythm
and her on lead on into the night
until, "I'm tired," she said, "and
it's time for bed." And I
knew by the way she said it
I wasn't included. So I
carefully kissed her goodbye
and the evening was over. I
haven't seen her since. She said
I made her angry and afraid.
Angry that I wasn't her ex-husband,
and afraid that I could be.
But I forgive her for those mistakes,
and now whenever I play,
I always see her
dark eyes cast down,
her smile, her blush, and

every song, blues or not,
is blues for her.

Camp

So here we sit cold
in the great brick house,
camped on an old
battlefield, leaning
on cracker boxes,
and burning rope
for warmth in the
wickless night. Then,
swaddled and curled
under fallen ensigns,
tapers waning like
flickering moons,
you and I at once
reverence tomorrow's
sun, the very pulpit sun
who, it is whispered,
will discard his
sermon notes and
bless us extempore.

Campaign

If I were general of your heart,
Commander-in-Chief of the militia of
your ante-bellum soul, we would
declare war on me and take me like
Grant took Richmond, by a
midnight march on the seat
of my capital C capitol. We would mine my
harbors and sink my ships. The struggle
would be affectionately fierce. After all,
I owe it to my men not to
capitulate too easily. But in the
end, especially in the end, I
the vanquished surrender
to us the unconditional, request the
there-are-no terms, and expect to be occupied for
a very long time. To the
victor belongs the spoils, and I am
both. Then comes Reconstruction.
That should happily detain
us for the rest of our little lives. And
finally, after our presidency, having
united again the disparate parts
of a great nation, and having conceived
at liberty and dedicated, we can navigate
Europe and re-invent New York,
and retire there to write
our memoirs, and joke
about who's buried
in our tomb.

Chairs

Quiet summer's day
at the lake. You and
I deep in lawn chairs
and conversation, about
nothing in particular.

The surface of the lake
shatters the sun into a
thousand pieces, each
piece wriggling on the
surface, a golden fish
unable to penetrate
the sky-blue meniscus.

But what is that to
us? Only a dance
of light. We have
our own dance, you
and I, to the orchestration
of the zephyr and the
choreography of the chimera.

If, as Artaud put it, actors
are athletes of the heart,
then lovers must be dancers
of the soul.

Chide Not

Chide not our dearest mother earth,
Nor ridicule her children nor her girth,
Nor take of something that to her belongs.
Else on the morrow at her behest,
Over you in her dank breast,
Will devils sing you to your rest,
With wild and melancholy songs!

Christmas Together

I have a dream
Of Christmas together
You and the kids
And me

I cry when I see
Again we're together
Santa's been good
To me

And on Christmas Eve
When little eyes go to sleep
I'll fall in love with you
One more time

I have a dream
It's Christmas forever
For you and the kids
And me

As long as I live
My love is forever
Here in my heart
You'll be

And under the tree
As far as the eye can see
Gifts of love to last
All our lives

I have a dream
Of Christmas together
You and the kids
And me

I cry when I see
Again we're together
Santa's been good
To me

Conflict

What is wrong with us?
If the world was at war,
we would be longing for
one another across continents,
hating the conflict that
had pulled us apart.
Me living in mud, and
waiting each day for
the letters you would
write at your walnut writing
table on scented stationery,
listening to the Mills
Brothers on the console
radio singing "Till Then."
And you'd pick up my
gold-framed uniform picture,
and kiss it tenderly as I
pull my pack from
the trench I slept in
last night, shouldering
my M-1 to march off
daydreaming of you
into machine gun fire
and bouncing bettys.

But the only war is
between you and me.
And the only deaths are
days dying slowly as
they pass. And the only
machine gun fire is on
a television special in
the living room. And the
only letters being written
are mine, giving you the
victory, and praying for

the time when I march
back home un-uniformed
and medal-less, and once
more into your arms.

Cords

"Cords?
You want hardwood cords do you?
I know where there's lots of black eye
oak maybe fifty cords of oak,"
I'm told by my friend. And even a woodcutter, even a part-time-
single-father-self-effacing-
with-two-very-young-children-and-not-surprised-with
this-life-woodcutter like me can figure out something like this-
that at some hundred and seventy-five dollars a cord that
sum of money'll do us good. "And it's all cut and stacked handsome
there," he says, "courtesy of the Forest Service as part of their
controlled cutting for forest fire control."
"Why don't you go get it for yourself," I ask? "Why?"
says he, "I don't wanna tear up my new four-wheel." Then he says,
"The wood is down the
thistle-thick side of this
almost vertical hill, not quite but almost
four hundred yards straight down. But that fifty-four
power wagon military ambulance of yours should have the power
to make it no problem. I'll show you where it is." So we leave to
drive about twelve miles down some dirt roads, and drive
out on the nob of what seems a small hill and he gets out
of his four wheel and I get out of
mine, and we walk a little ways to where the calamine
colored road overlooks a deep col,
and the road falls and tumbles over and
all the way off the nob like a dusty ribbon falling off a wall.
"The oak's down there," he says squatting and staring down into the
little canyon beneath us. "Of course, a little
of it might be pine but most of
it is ready-to-split
oak." "What oak?"
I say, staring down too with squint in my eye.
And he points out tiny gray cubes, and
they're way at the bottom near a tiny stream. "That oak there
looks a hell of a lot further down just now than it looks

at first to me," I say, "I don't know if I can flat
get down there much less get
out." "This road," he says, "was carved out about
four years ago by Forest Service bulldozers for
clearing those trees." And he pauses, clearing
his throat and staring down into the canyon, his
eyes squinting to half size.
"All I ask," he says standing up, "is by fall
that you bring me a couple of complimentary cords that
I can burn myself this winter." "Okay," says I,
working on trying not to remember how much hard work
loading and unloading
a complimentary cord of oak can be. "Well, I gotta go to a
job, a $2500 carpet job,"
he says, and grins and climbs in. He
drives his new four-wheel off the nob and I watch him drive
away, leaving me confronting fortune a mere quarter-mile away.
As I start down the precipice in as
lowly a gear as I have, I remember having dreams about driving slowly
on highways so steep my car would flip on
over the top, and I think my truck might flip on over
at any moment now. Just outside my door is flat
out freefall to the bottom of the canyon, and I'm devout
in my wish for my door to remain in
the closed position. But soon I'm actually at the bottom of the
oak canyon, not so little from down here, and I'm agape at oak
cut and stacked for acres, and each a perfect 22 inch cut.
I'm chicken-counting delirious, and in my head I'm
already spending the thousands I'll get for all
the wood as I'm loading the
first load on my truck, until I've loaded a cord. First
I close the doors on the back of the ambulance, and then I
ascend in the kickass
lowest and slowest
of granny gears. We climb the side of
the cliff and all goes smoothly, until halfway up, right at the
part of the road where a small downhill dirt rampart
on the passenger side drops off into oblivion.

The steepness of the climb here, coupled with the
ton of wood in the back, causes my front wheels to spin wanton
and careless in the high desert dust, and
now we are no longer climbing very well at all. Now,
driving up a very steep incline in a four-wheel drive
with a ton of wood in the back is one thing, but what with
all the stopping and starting I now do on that incline, all
that wood begins to have certain ideas of its own that
involve banging open one of the back doors and falling in
a growing heap behind me. Yes, and if it grows at a
not unexpected pace for the next five minutes, then I may not
have any wood left by the time I get to the road's top half.
Now that I'm stopped what now?
Can't seem to go up. Can't
turn around. Could get out and walk away and never return.
Or, and it's a big or,
I can pick up the fallen wood, back down this cliff of a hill and try
to get some momentum to
get back up. There's only one problem—what gear to get
back down in, first or reverse. If I back
down in reverse, then how to do it without the truck rolling down
granny-free and gone, because if I miss the reverse-same-as-granny
gear, my brakes will never stop me. But reverse is the gear,
so I manage to shift cleanly, or at least reasonably so,
and begin backing down this high-desert scrub and sand
Matterhorn using only side mirrors until mirrors don't matter.
And when I hit land, and
I am at the bottom again after a sudden eternity, I
kiss the ground and get an earthy pebble-and-twig kiss
back. Now to unload the wood and try to back
out of here. But I'm stopped again backing out
right where I was before, but at least now I'm facing the right
way, if the right way is down. So once more I crawl my way
down the hill, and not for the last time up or down.
All day I try, full and empty, and as oaken shadows fall
I realize my predicament. I must walk out. So I
follow the stream waters that follow
the canyon in one direction or another, and of course it's the

two-mile-walk-over-moss~covered-rocks-until-you-get-to-
a-dirt-road scenario. Then it's a
long walk on a dark road, until a truck driver comes along,
whiskeyed up enough to agree to whisk
me into a town close by, but so far away it feels like Miami.
Come next day, my friend with the new four wheel has to come
pull me out of that canyon and let his new truck set an example.
And he's impatient and he pushes it too hard, and
he sort of burns up his clutch in the process. He's
not speaking to me much lately. I hope he's not
really still counting on those complimentary
cords.

Creamery

Working with him,
Saturday mornings from eight till noon,
sometimes I'd ride my Lambretta
to the shop (Remember one time you
almost lost me when the engine
froze at fifty, locking the back
wheel, and I just missed that
telephone pole?) from the house by
Quito School, all the way to Palo Alto.
I felt so grown up with my own
machine, whether the scooter started or
not, which half the time it didn't. I
painted it myself, had the motor apart
by myself, but needed his help putting it
back together. (Remember when you, no,
my stepfather, helped me buy that Austin
Healy with the spare engine in the trunk,
and the loose rear wheel, and the wiring
so crossed that hitting the brake pedal turned
on the headlights?) Those four hours on
Saturday mornings seemed eternity itself,
a hundred glances at the clock until coffee
break time, when we'd walk to the snack shack
or drive to the creamery lunch counter,
so I could smile at the counter girl. (Remember
her name, do you, I don't, who finally asked about
me after I had gone to Connecticut that summer?)
Then back to the shop for another interminable two
hours (Remember how you always gave me the worst
work, thank you?) scraping oil pan sludge and bottom,
scouring gaskets from heads, holding trannies
on my stomach like iron lovers, while he
bolted them down in a kind of father and son,
nepotistic threesome, metallic group grope.
(Remember those outlines of the tools you
had me paint on the board where they hung,

where the paint dripped and dried, reminding
me for years I shouldn't hope to be the
artist that you should have been?) There were the
constant stream of visitors to the shop, the
bosses in their sterile suits asking for work
on their personal vehicles, the milk truck
drivers confessing their mechanical slash
marital problems, the parts house guys from
next door with shit to shoot, the glass shop
owner down the alley way with a Chevy to sell.
(Remember, no, I guess I never told you,
how much a part of me those once
discarded, disregarded Saturdays still are
that aren't?) Funny how we love what we hated, and
miss now what we never dreamed we had. (Remember
that you said working in grease made you look
younger because it kept your hair from turning
white?) And now I know, it was the discovery of a
part of myself that I would never have made without
sweating in the semi-clean coveralls with his
name on the pocket. (Remember the almost hospital
smell of the little washroom where we washed
up at work's end, next to the compressor that would
start suddenly and scare the hell out of me and
make you laugh?) And if there is a moral, if there
is to be a neat wrapping up of what I learned
those years of Saturdays from eight till noon, it
is this: get life under your fingernails so
it never comes out, not with hand cleaner, not
with nail files, not with death. (Remember why,
without you, I used to drive past the cemetery
where her seventeen years were buried on
my way home, never stopping at the grave?)
I can't recall the last Saturday I worked. No
brass band played to mark its passing. No
gold watch was given in thanks for half a
decade of Saturday service. No one said goodbye
with a tear in his eye, or a lump in his throat,

or a hand extended. (Remember, not even you?)
And now I know, yes, now I know, that every day
is hello for the first time and goodbye for the last.
Every day is wiping the grease from our faces and
the blood from our torn fingers. Every day is
making the trucks run one more day with
baling wire and coffee cans of nuts and bolts.
Every day is smiling at the girl behind the
creamery counter, and not remembering the
first time I saw her for the very last time.

Creature

I've seen you only
so many times, only so
many French scenes –
you entering the restaurant, you
leaving, you pulling up to the dance
club riding with your friend, you
dancing, you exiting, you standing already
in the bar, me walking
you out. But forget those trifles,
and dance with me again. Fasten
me again with your eyes, those
tender rivets. Talk to me again,
under the music, ear to my brain.
Let me curl your hand to my chest
as we sway, two ships on high seas.
Let me feel your breath on my face,
like the Philippine wind on a Luzon
beach years ago, where the natives
told me of a sea creature so poisonous,
that to be bitten by it was to die in thirty
seconds, but so small that the only place
it could bite you was the skin between
your fingers. And now all I can say is,
you've bitten my heart between its
fingers, and I'm counting down the
seconds until I succumb to you.

Cry3

She never cries in front of me. Although
when she's alone, maybe a tear finds its
way
down
her Mother Mary face, to
kiss the pink rose lips I left so
many kisses shy. Strength
is a strange thing, sometimes
a giving in, sometimes a
determination, sometimes
a refusal to resign, sometimes
a resignation. Sometimes maybe
the loneliest tear on the
sweetest face after I'm
gone.

Dear Silly and Quirky

Dear Silly and Quirky,
Flawless perfection here. I found
your profile alternately fascinating
and devastating. Fascinating
because I too have given up meeting
people in bars, and behind bars too.
Devastating because your angel smile
has challenged my long-held belief
that such a vision could only be
found in paintings by the masters,
or in eye-care professional outlets.
Really though, and all seriousness
aside, I feel you and I could make
beautiful music together, kinda like a
kazoo chorus with each kazoo
tuned to a different note. What a
meaningful coincidence that you
live by your art and I live by mine.
Mine lives two doors down. Perhaps,
though, someone like me can replace
your art. I'll be your pallet and your
brush, your treble clef and your g-string,
your cello and your Monticello, your
Sistine chapel and your velvet Elvis
painting. And I'm handy with words
too, like vociferous and coniferous
and antidisestablishmentarianism.
So if your syntax ever breaks down,
I can fix it. But enough about me
and more about me. I adore you
and a window you. Can I say that yet?
I want to spend the rest of my life
with you, or at least a week or two.
By then you'll probably be sick
of me, or at least want to put a
contract out on me. I had a cat

put out on me once, but never mind
that. So I guess my question is,
who are you now and who were you
then, and who said I had a question
anyway? From now on I'll just let
my guitar do the talking, and boy
can it dominant a chordversation.
Hoping to hear from you soon,
so we can start living together
in bledded wiss or just in sin,
if you have no objections. I know
I don't. And you won't either after
I work my magic on you. Okay, pick
a card, any card. On second thought,
forget that and watch me pull a hat
out of my rabbit. On third thought,
let's get back to the living in sin part.
Your most reverent admirer,
signed, The Irreverent Admirer.
P.S. Oh nothing, I just couldn't tear
myself away from you yet.

Dippledy Doodledy

Dippledy doodledy
Apple Figstrudley
Ate while he rode on a
Dappled young mare.
Somehow he overlooked
Branch-hanging-lowly-down,
Now he'll take lunch on a
Bruised derriere.

Hocuso pocuso
Hilda Katrinideau
Cast forty spells in a
Pique of blind rage.
Slaking her thirst for the
Unquenchifiable,
Chomped she the heads off of
Bats in a cage.

Hoggletug poggletug
Magnified Woggle Bug
Thoroughly educates
People of Oz.
Once you have met him you're
Incontrovertibly
Stunned by the size of his
Brain and his schnoz.

Pepper hot piper snot
Peterkin Paperbot
Laughed when he saw an old
Lady fall through.
He didn't know she was
Extraterrestrial,
Now he plays pipe in a
Cold Martian zoo.

Don't Do It

Don't give honey to young babies
Don't give baubles to a queen
Don't sell toy boats to the navies
And don't fall in love with me

Don't eat pesticided daisies
Don't get X-rays twice a week
Don't try scratchin' itchy scabies
And don't fall in love with me

Don't get blown away by breezy
Don't ride saddles out to sea
Don't make sandwiches too cheesy
And don't fall in love with me

Don't trade hard for way too easy
Don't start runnin' when you pee
Don't take cliff roads if you're queasy
And don't fall in love with me

Don't do it
Just don't do it

Dr. Livingstone, I Presume

Every smile, every slashing
hip, every rainbow eye of hers
that lands on me like
a flitting tropical butterfly,
confirms in my heart
what rapacious lovers
seek to prove in the
jungles of each other's arms.
But I must wait for her
as she discovers herself.
So I who would love her the most,
the future explorer of her
rainforests and cartographer of
her waterfalled wildernesses
and free soloer of her mantled peaks,
wait patiently, lying on my back
in my base camp of dreams,
hands behind my head,
contemplating constellations as her face
for however long she may take.

Dreams

I dreamed of you from
before, in flights of blue
unconsciousness, the first time
and the last.

Striding through the door,
confident in your precariousness,
you hardly glanced
my way. But I remembered you from
the primeval night when you
touched my arm with the fingertips
of gathering centuries,
outside reaching in.

It was an aching
search but I have found you
again. Don't you recognize me?
Have I changed so much in the millenniums, while
the envious eons have been so kind to
you despite your struggles?
Life is always full
of struggles. How many deaths
have we died to live
to be together?

Don't be frightened now. It's
only me.

Duke

"Do you have a cell phone, mister?"

"Not on me. Why, son?"

"Because my dog Duke got loose and I can't catch him by myself, and I want to call my parents. We just live down the street."

"Yeah, he'll run into the road if you're not careful. I'll help you. Grab his collar!"

"Oh Duke!"

"Sneak up on him son. Come here, Duke! Duke! Get out of the road!! Oh!!"

"Duke!!"

"You almost got it there, Duke, six inches from that back wheel…"

"Please, Duke."

"The car tried to stop because he heard me yell. He never even saw him."

"Come here Duke. Please, Duke."

"Excuse me sir, do you have a cell phone?"

"No? Well would you mind helping this boy and me catch his dog? Thanks. He almost just got run over, so keep him away from the road. Don't let him get by you."

"Sometimes he comes if I lie down."

"Okay son. Try it. Lie down on the grass."

"Come on Duke. Please Duke."

"Okay, catch him son! Oh, almost. Dive on him when he comes close again. We can't do this all night. It's already getting dark."

"Come on, Duke. Please, Duke."

"Dive on him!"

"Please, Duke!"

"Oh you do? Later then, and thanks for trying to help, sir. Okay, try lying down again, son. That seemed to get him to come closer to you. Okay grab him, son! Alright! Now, don't let go! You almost had a dead dog, so don't let go. How far down are you?"

"All the way down by the light."

"That is a ways. Sorry I don't have a car. If you get tired of walking bent over, then sit down and rest, but don't let go of him."

"Why'd that other guy laugh? It wasn't funny."

"Well, it was son, with Duke running around in circles like that. Zooming by you. He was glad to be free and playing with us. What might have happened wasn't funny, that Duke almost got run over. But Duke is funny."

"Mm."

"See you later son. Keep a tight fist on that collar."

The next day.

"Duke! Tied to a tree? What have they done to you, Duke? Remember me, Duke? Last night I helped catch you and save your life. Duke, you little brown and white rascal! Don't pull so hard on that leash to get at me Duke, you'll choke yourself."

Explorers

She explores my bed
like early man crossing
the land bridge from Asia
to North America on foot for
the first time. "I hadn't
planned on being here," she
says, slipping off her jeans
with a little help from me.
"You don't have to be," I say,
tugging her shirt up over
her silken hair. "I want you
to be comfortable and happy."
"I am," she says, setting out
across my body like Norsemen
over new seas in brave open
boats. "I want to help you know
the truth about yourself," I say, "to
help you understand just how
beautiful you are." "Maybe you
already have," she says, grasping
me hard like an Arctic admiral
planting his country's flag in
thick ice at the pole. "Ohhh," I say,
long-drawing out the word, as
would an Old World potentate
upon learning a lush New World
has just been claimed in His Name.

Fall Was Never So

Fall was never so
splendid as she.
There are more rainbows
in her hair than jack frost
has colors on his palette – more
October sunsets in her smile
than in the accumulated
history of countless worlds.

Pastel leaves sought her
shoulders like garish garlands,
trying too hard to be beautiful
beside her. The clever wind ran
slender fingers through her
raven hair under the total
pretense of frivolity, when
actually it was seeking any
excuse just to brush her cheek.

The sun sent streaming
rays to discover what truth
really meant, but she blinded
them with a smile, and they
scattered to distant corners
of the universe and hid, rather
than confess that the merest
sparkle of her eyes is greater
than ten thousand galactic suns.

Fifty

The months unfold
like wet envelopes,
oozing their epistles
of goo on the flea market
fiesta platter I chose so
carefully in my dream
for us back then, when
we were old and coupled.
Now the loneliness of
youth courses sullenly
through my veins. Or is it
arteries? You would know,
nurse of my heart.
Dreams are never real,
just Burma Shave signs
on a California desert
road a quarter century ago,
when I was the hope
of the human race and
the fantasy of middle-
aged dance instructors.
How was I to know,
how could I ever know
then, that one day I
would love you, but you
would need your anger
so much more than
you ever needed me?

Final Score

six billion tons –
six billion tons of toxic waste each year

Yaaaay!

if one ton was a yard cubed,
who could say, maybe it's more –
a 60,000 x 100,000 yard area one yard high
that's approximately 35 miles wide and 58 miles long
not fenced off and guarded day and night
in some obscure corner of the globe
if globes have corners
by armed serious men who don't seem
to know any better than to be working next to,
or in, a carcinogenic cesspool
no not that

Fumble!

but spread here among our children
on their little smiles
taken orally and gustatorally
into their big hearts
here in the air you breathe
and the water you drink, no
that bottle won't protect you,
won't shield you from what piece
is yours of that 6 billion tons, and
how much does it take to kill me?
you know they never even cared to
try to to take the smallest amount of
time to try and figure that out

Touchdown!

35 miles wide and 58 miles long every year

every single year for say a decade,
so in the last decade, if
it were stored together in a safe place,
but it's not,
then in the last decade it will have
grown to be an area the size of
new hampshire

Interception, and it's going the other way!

so that's the equivalent of
one state we would have completely
covered in noxious substance, completely
unlivable except for the guy
sitting farther down the bar
who says he'll live anywhere

Fumble!

but it's not like that
the stuff sleeps with you at night
and goes to school with the
children, and when they get
to school it's already there
waiting to take their coat
and slip inside their noses
and begin killing them
like it's killing you and
me

Safety!

and you know the amount and
the effects are under reported and
under studied, and under the table
so we know it's more and we know
it's soon and we know it's deadly
but…

they'll keep giving it to us
a thimbleful at a time, but plenty
still, for the likes of us, human and alive

remember the cancer that ray died of,
and the alzheimers that martha lost herself to,
and the stroke that paddy had, and the heart
attack that took dow, don't you think that
a lot, or at least some, of that comes from
that new hampshire sized patch of deadly goo,
that is not goo and
is not in new hampshire,
that they have spread among all of us?
don't you think that had anything to do with
the cost of health and the cost of life,
just so a few careless individuals could
put more money into their pockets?
they don't even have to test the six
billion tons, and that's just what they throw
away

they don't even have to test what they
sell to us

not <u>really</u> test because
why should they care?

Touchdown!

Final score…

Foolishness

The sky and I sailed out to sea today.
The sea got up and dripping slipped away.
We followed her into a bar in town.
She picked a fight with desert-loving clowns.
She broke them, crashed them, drove them to the ground.
They fell like foam and never made a sound.
She chugged her drink and sloshed on out the door.
The glowing screen replayed it slow once more.
We helped her give her sandy room a sweep.
Then silently she settled down to sleep.
The sky and I trudged grudgingly outside.
Since he was headed home I bummed a ride.

Four Wheels and a Desert Flower

Gripping the steering wheel
with the index and middle fingers
of my hand resting casually on
my leg, I drive the '54 Dodge
Power Wagon military ambulance
towards what to my lovely passenger
looks like a wall of smooth
rock obelisking in front of us.
Pausing before this seemingly
insurmountable barrier, I put
the transfer case in low and
shift into granny gear top
speed four miles per hour. "You're
not going over that!?" is the
question. "Done it many times,"
is the answer, and I press
the issue and the accelerator and
let out on the shiny metal clutch
pedal, flush with inexorability, as
the front end of the four-ton four-
by-four begins to climb, taking us
quickly to a near ninety degree
angle, seemingly, though not
actually, vertical. And somehow
the truck keeps climbing like a
ponderous fly, until now all we
can see is sky and the noonday sun
in our eyes. And somehow the truck
keeps climbing. Now we seem
suspended above the earth, and she
begins to scream. But I can't stop here,
and somehow the truck keeps
climbing to its castle keep, and crests
the ridge, now seen to be about twenty
feet high and not very much shy of
vertical. The road leaps over, and

pirouettes around, and stumbles over
the high desert stubbled with
severe hills. She stops screaming
long enough to admire the view
and catch a breath, before we at a
plunging crawl descend the gnarled
ribbon to a new chorus of screams,
and me with a wicked smile on
my entirely innocent face.

Fridays

Did you see me
waiting for you in
the entry hall, defying the
indiscriminate warmth of the relentless
hostess-food-service-hooker? (What
shot, slug, hit, puff, upper, does she
need to greet me like that?) Two
women with a stroller and a baby
ask if there is room for the stroller
inside. (Yes but not for the baby, I
answer silently.) Non smoking? (No,
smoking please, I want to start
the baby off early.) Through the
glass a pretty dark-haired woman,
a Snow White after the dwarves,
speaks silently to a child I
cannot see, or else condescends
to a very small adult, one of the
leftover dwarves perhaps. I
fancy myself the Prince kissing
her in her glass coffin. (Would she
cough up apple into my kiss?) The
door opens again and my wait
is over. Now we can accept the
hostess' habitual hospitality.
Now we can be seated, you and I
and your son, almost three is he?
Reminds me of one of my sons.
(Reminds me of me, oh that reminds me.)
Today I gladly trade Snow White and
her diminutive invisible friend for
you and innocent Isaac. Could I be
Abraham? No, the only sacrifice
today will be my heart to your
green eyes. (I didn't know they
grew emeralds in Ohio.) Shall we order?

Gas Station Restroom

There were times he thought
Of leavin' this world
With its effed up leaders
And its millions of churls

But the bridge was too high
And the knife too sharp
And the AR too messy
And he's afraid of the dark

It wasn't that folks didn't like him
It wasn't that he wasn't fun
Alright, so they didn't like him
Alright, so he wasn't fun

But still is that any reason
He should be rejected
Subjected
Objected
Imperfected
Bi-sected

As if he's not one of the gang
He don't belong to their club
They all just doin' their thing
And he's feelin' the snub

They're dancin' to music
He's never heard
And the language they're speakin'
He don't know a word

It's the saddest story you'll ever hear
Until you hear a sadder one
It's the baddest tale you'll ever be told
Until you're told a badder one

On a dismal night in June
Clouds slapped at the face of the moon
The bottom fell out too soon
In a gas station restroom

There were times he felt on top of the world
There were times when the world was on him
There were times he thought he'd crawl
Out from under, and get back in the swim

On a rainy night in June
Clouds spit in the face of the moon
And the bottom fell out too soon
In a gas station restroom
Not exactly the Louvre
Or even Gilley's
Just a back station restroom
A gas station restroom

The moral to this story
If moral can be had
Is that morals are only what you think
And there ain't much to that

In with the good air
And out with the bad

On a dismal night in June
Clouds scratched at the face of the moon
And the bottom came up too soon
In a gas station restroom

Clouds punched at the face of the moon
And the end came too soon
In a gas station restroom

Gaslight

Right around the corner
from Dave and Kathy's midtown bungalow,
I climb the careful concrete steps,
undaunted by the warning signs
for the under 30 crowd, and
slide myself squeaky onto
a black stool barside at
the Gaslight Café, where
Sandy serves German beer and
sparkling wisdoms interspersed
with sagacious smiles. I
feed the jukebox dollars for
the questionable privilege
of tapping an Adidas to well-worn
hits spinning in and out of key,
as Sandy's eyes dance to distractions,
other men and other beers and
a fresh helping of ruby red
lipstick judiciously applied,
but unnecessary. Because if a
man gets past her eyes in
less than a month of Mondays, he's either
spending every waking hour at the Gaslight,
or really just not paying attention.

Gone

Touch the aloe plant
that she last touched.
Close the bedroom door
that she left open.
Turn off the scattering light
that she turned on.
Or maybe no.
Let it shine a little,
little longer, only
one more hour or so.

Kiss the brown clay cup
that she last kissed.
Sing the sea wind song
that she sang leaving.
Draw up the clattering sheets
that she pressed down.
Or maybe no.
Let them lie a little,
little longer, only
one more hour or so.
Who will know?

Good Kills

Lordy, heck of a day. Good kills. – NY Times

An old man lies face up in the road
near the Diyala River bridge,
never to grow older,
April 6, Baghdad,
things are going really well,
with a hole in his head,
bloating like a Matthew Brady,
establishing a violent supremacy.
his cane of aluminum,
a king's ransom in another time,
My men showed no mercy today,
outstanding!
lying impoverished by his side,
needing him to stand.
Better safe than sorry.
And there are others,
Don't use my name, I don't want
my children to know what I do.
cars full of corpses, corpses of children
and women killed today.
When we tell them to stop,
they have to stop.
They were trying to find
How can you tell? You can't tell.
a safe place to go.
What were they doing in a taxi
in the middle of a war zone?
The flies on the children's eyes,
Half of their soldiers look like civilians.
gorge without grace.
You can't blame Marines,
there's nothing we could do.
In the road near the Diyala River bridge,
an old man lies face up.

Harbor

She spoke of storms,
and the marina boats,
sleepy-eyed under the cool September moon,
nodded gently at their moorings.
She spoke of husbands and fathers,
and the color-soaked sky,
crushed with the loss of the day,
flooded the pale dining deck in scarlet.
She spoke of journeys,
and in my mind I sailed beside her
where I had never been,
upon courageous ancient seas.
And her eyes thundered
and her smile flashed,
setting fire to the night.
And as the conflagration raged,
my heart held out its mariner hands
to warm them.

Help

Dear *Miss Advice on Love*:
Once I met a girl who ended
all her sentences like this!
And this?? And sometimes even this!!!
And would you believe this!!?
Whereas I (I like to use parenthetical
statements alot) usually would end
sentences much in this manner. Or this?
Or sometimes even this! But never this!!?
However, now (I think everyone
should use parenthetical statements more
frequently) that I have gotten to know
this girl (I call her a girl and I think all
women should call themselves girls
and insist that men do too and
should use parenthetical statements
more frequently), I find that with ever
increasing regularity, I am ending my
sentences like this!! Or this!? And
(oh yes!) today I found myself
wanting to use this!!! at the end
of a sentence!!! Imagine!!!! I
said imagine!!!!! And now I'm
wondering (I think that the connotation
of wondering ((wonder being a chronic
upcropping of the Latin syntactical
anomaly, wondorphulis)) serves no!!!
((I repeat no!!!)) sociological purpose
whatsofreakingever!?!?), I'm really
beginning to wonder,,,,,,
Do??? I need!!!!!!!
Professional help!!?!?!?!!?!?!?!!?!?!?
!!?!?!?!!?!?!?!!?!?!?!!?!?!?!!?!?!?!!
?!?!?!!?!?!?!!*$#*~%
Sincerely,
%#"&%#@#%&$&x(*~q

In the Madness

In the madness,
the woman writhes
and screams and gasps
and grasps the crook
of death's arm, as her
panicked fellows help
her to a Humvee and
hurry her to an ebbing
dream, shortened by
a limb or by a lifetime.

In the madness,
those whose follies
put young women
in a soldier's gear to fill
a stranger's gun sights
and slow the shrapnel
from an equal opportunity
rocket-powered grenade
for the slick of oil that
is their acres of ranches
and their pickups and
their caviars and their
careers and their wives'
designer gowns, joke
and mechanically savor
their lead crystal
goblets of rare wine,
blood-red and flowing
freely like the
end of the woman's
severed arm.

In the madness,
you and I turn
our shame away,

and say that that
is life and there is
nothing we can do,
and isn't the weather
cool today, and aren't
the gas prices high, while
a politician who never
earned a nickel by the
sweat of his own brow,
speaks to us about how
freedom isn't free,
and about how the
sacrifices of our young
men and women are
making the world safe
for a democracy that,
in the end it seems,
exists only for those
who can afford to have
others pay the price.

January Road

Sleeted streets seem to be the light.
Snow on the van's rack holds the
used-to-dangle gas cap while I pump.
Still thinking of you,
I pull the nozzle out,
and let the fluid drip lazily
from tip to tank, as
skies promise more fleecy flakery,
and the air sculpts my breath in vanilla frosting.
Vaguely, I eavesdrop on the ocean
ever-caressing rocks into sand
as it does all night, and all nights.
The steering wheel is cold between my fingers,
but it warms as I imagine it to be
your gloved hand.

Joking

Wasn't
bus eleven so yellow all our yesterdays, those bus
stop mornings? And if she doesn't stop
being so damn sexy. And if she wasn't being
somebody else's wife. Somebody
I like. I
remember the milky mornings. I remember
snowflakes falling on her hyacinth hair as snow
white tiny diadems. I begged requite
for mercy skyward, silently, four
times, and swore if I ever met her once, just one time
in the dark, I would kiss her in
earnest, and somehow that would flame the unfurnaced
for both of us. For
I know she's thought of it too, and why.
But she hides it well, never overtly flirting, but
only just giving only
indication enough, so I know she (my vindication)
hears, and that my ironies don't fall on escallonia ears.
"If you see my husband in your travels... if
you see my husband with another woman," she joked, "you
better let me know." I smiled and said, "You bet,
and if he is, can I have you?" She laughed, and
"Sure," she said, "sure,"
still joking. I still
wasn't.

Lafayette's Bed

We marched the
labyrinth of Hartford,
she and I and
fascination, taking museums and
stalking soup,
chasing dichromic glass,
and flanking bread and
Trinity and Twain, and
Lafayette's battle bed.

We halted over Lafayette's
bed (really an adjustable cot),
and wondered if he could
see us in a dream 220
years ago. Of course, he'd
look at her first, only naturally,
and then at me. But then, if he
looked at her first, he might
never get to me. He might be
overcome with the thought
that somehow he has died
in his sleep, and an angel has
arrived to escort him to Paradise.
But we're only in an old state
house. And Lafayette's bed is
enclosed in a glass case. And
she is better than angels.

Afterwards, we sailed over
lawns and grounds, and
glided under great red oaks
to hear a thousand birds sing.
She threw leaves at me
from behind a mischievous
smile, and I returned both
compliments, while
Lafayette dreamed.

Lament for My Father

I never got to hold you,
there at your life's end,
to sit by your bed and
take your withered hand
in mine, or put my head
on your still, thin shoulder
and leave tear marks on
your long, fragile sleeve.

For some reason,
I imagine you there
as you slipped away,
wearing the same shirt
you wore in all those
pictures from your twenties.
Yes, the reddish plaid shirt
you wore in all those pictures,
as if it were, more than likely,
the only dressy one you had.

I should have been there,
even though you wouldn't,
you couldn't, have heard
me, falling deeper into
the lasting sleep like you were.
It's only for me that I regret
the lack of goodbyes or,
more painful still
for both of us, the years
of the lack of hellos.

The sky wore a blue shirt today
in your memory,
not plaid. And all I can think
is that it was, more than likely,
the only dressy one it had.

Last Valentine

Last Valentine's Day
I didn't even really know you,
and now on this one, I wake in the morning
and sit in a chair beside your harbor window
overlooking centenarian docks, and a trio of
moored maroon tugboats, and outdoor
restaurants with the chairs and stools
all gone, draped in winter white,
and buoys on the river red
and yellow like floating
pointed party hats,
and wish that you will be
my latest, and in a far-off year
yet to come,
my last Valentine.

Listen

"No one listens,"
she protested, but
I heard porcelain ships
shelling our little songs.
"They didn't listen
when I said I didn't
want to meet anyone new,"
she insisted, but I heard
spotted clocks gnawing on the
underbelly of our happiness.
"You never listen,"
she blurted finally.
But I heard the children
sleeping, and the old house
creaking, and the dream
choking there beside us
in the thin night.

Little Yellow Football

It didn't last long. I
remember throwing it
away years after it had
gone through the window,
cracked and yellow, the
little yellow football.
It was harder than
the window that it
flew through on an
errant pass from me.
Neither lasted very
long, window or
football, but they have
lasted longer, much longer,
in the stories that are
told when my
brother and I get
together. But who
will tell stories of us
when we are cracked
and yellow, and who
will throw us away?

Midnight

Channel flipping...
cable surfing...
waiting for the eyes
of the woman I love.
Headline news... fitness
equipment... infomercial...
weather over Iowa...
Christopher Lee horror film...
fast-talking stand-up comedian...
World War II...
the Phil Silvers Show...
beautiful woman's breasts...
Yankees vs...
beautiful woman's breasts.
Indoor soccer...
live hernia operation...
insipid Hollywood gossip...
World War II again... beautiful
woman's breasts. U.S. Open tennis...
beautiful woman's breasts.
The eyes of the woman I love!
Home from shopping...
the woman I love's
hand on my knee... makeup infomercial...
beautiful woman's breasts... tv
suddenly going off... lights going off...
the eyes of the woman I love
pushing me down...
kissing me all over...
really close
beautiful woman's breasts.

New Blue Shoes

Today I bought them
each a pair of new blue shoes.
They were so proud
to prance about the store
glancing at themselves in mirrors,
a self-conscious smile creeping
over one little face,
a wide grin always
on the other.
We were shopping
because one old pair of shoes
was outgrown,
like the love between you and me.
And the other pair
was broken,
like the three hearts
shopping without you,
for new blue shoes.

No Towel Is Safe

No towel is safe from you,
so they hide in strange closets
with faraway linens and other
less cherry terry cloths, until you
find them and throw them mercilessly
wet upon the flippant floor.
But the coffee cups now, they love you!
Each repeatedly accorded his own
ride of joy, tumbling between the
seats of the van, flying through
the air to perish happily on ocean-
gathered rocks, rocking joyously as
waves of creamy brown break lastingly
upon the ubiquitous whatever whites.

Nor'easter

I brave the beach
in a storm that a
few others only wish
to experience from the
inside of their vehicles.
But the sea spray
is my vehicle and
the slick round rocks
my bald tires and
the howling wind my
anxious lover, running
her ecstatic hands
roughly through my
seaweed hair as we
motor, tugging at my
buttons, sliding her
cold wet tongue into
my ear, drumming
a thousand knuckles
on the dashboard of
clouds, eager to get
me alone and show
me all her wetness.
But the waves are
chaperones, reaching out
with briny fingers
to separate us and climb
between us on the
thick stone loveseat
that the sea has carved
just in time, anticipating
our lighthouse romance
by ten million centuries.

Oh No

Oh no.
The cats have caught another bird.
Despite the fact that the cats are confined to the porch,
every now and then they catch a bird that wanders in.
It's still alive, lying on its side, breathing,
its mouth opening and closing without a sound.
That's it, goes my inner conversation,
this means another trip to the Center for Wildlife,
who take such good care of injured creatures,
to leave to them the hope of saving this bird's life,
unlike the one the cats got last year. But the year before
that we brought them a nest full of dying baby birds that
the cats had nothing to do with, and despite having
to feed them every hour for two weeks,
they saved them all.
But today I put the bird in a shoebox, still on its side,
still breathing, its sad bird mouth still opening and closing.
Yes, I'll make the drive to the Center. I can't just let it die.
Make the phone call and tell them we're coming, and
check on the bird in the hope that something miraculous
has happened. But no, still lying on its side,
breathing, mouth opening and closing.
I put on my coat, and bring a towel to the box
to cover the bird. But the bird has moved to the
other corner of the box. Now this is a hopeful sign,
and I take my coat off. But the bird just sits there
in the other corner of the box for the longest time.
Well, it's forty five minutes to the center and who
knows how much longer this bird really has,
so I reach in cover it gently with the towel and
interlock the cardboard over it for the trip to the Center.
And it flies away.
The next day I find a half-dead mouse that the cats
have brought in from the garage, and I
toss it out into the backyard.

Out of State Plates

So, inadvertently, I
followed her into a
Poconos WalMart parking lot
late one Thursday night,
actually just about midnight.
I didn't even know for
sure if she was a he or a her,
she sat slumped so low
in the seat. But I did notice
the Alabama plates. So
when she pulled into the
lot, I parked not far away,
not out of sight, but out of
curiosity, with the thought
that it might very well be a
pretty Alabama lady. Then the
door of her car opened
about six inches, and I noticed
it as I walked toward the store's
triple doors, all automatic
opening and made of
glass, which they cover with
stickers. (So I ask you, why
make a door of glass if you
are going to cover the glass
with stickers? The automatic
part is nice, though, if
only it wasn't delayed quite
so much that if you walk
forward briskly enough,
you have to pause in
your stride for a half second
or else walk face first into
the doors.) Anyway, Alabama
plates' door opens all the way
now, and a heart-melting young

lady gets out in a blonde ponytail
and a long-sleeve shirt with the tails
hanging out over indiscriminately
baggy pants of indeterminate
style. But she's completely beautiful.
So I walk slower, so that we
get to the store doors at almost
the same time, and we do. And
unlike most Pennsylvania women
she looks at me, a stranger, and
smiles, and her lips are devastatingly
soft even from five feet away. And
even though I can't see the color of
her eyes, they're blue I guarantee
you. They'd have to be, because a
sun that bright needs a very blue
sky. Then she walks ahead of
me, and I watch her walk and wonder
if I shouldn't contrive some reason
to follow. But, I figure, if it's
"right" then we'll meet again. But
we don't, and I leave the store with
a vague but persistent sense of life
passing me by, as I pass by the little
white car with the Alabama plates.
What would it have hurt to try to
get to know her better? To say
something like, "So, are you the
one from Alabama?" And if so,
then maybe something like, "So
what are you doing here in PA,
for God's sake?" And when I'm
ninety, and can't read out of state
plates if you hold them in front
of my fizzled face, will I wish that
I had carped the diem and not just let
her walk away, even if I'm obviously
slightly over forty and she's obviously

slightly over twenty? Because when
I'm seventy she'll be forty some, and
maybe thinking about some young man
she followed into a store parking lot, and
maybe dealing with a vague but
persistent feeling of life passing
her by sporting out of state plates.

Party

After a
light rain, she takes flight
and flits from sand
flower to jungle flower,
looking smoother than hummingbirds look,
and with narrower hips. Her grand
pendulant pendant carving each half open
white breast, like the whitest
Hershey chocolate for a new year's morning. Her
arm brushes mine meticulously, no harm –
earnestly the softest skin I could learn.
Inevitably, she is rococo porcelain,
nowhere more than here on slender legs. Now
rain again, heavier rain.

Pears

"Be careful you
don't step on the pears,"
she warned as I weaved
my way across her little
yard, past the pear tree,
somehow wiser than fruit
trees are supposed to be,
and smug, even as if it
had heard those words many
thousands of times before. "My
mother," she said, as I climbed
blue back porch steps to
her kitchen, "used to make me
pick up pears when I was
a little girl, before I could
do the fun things I wanted
to do, and I hated it." And
looking back through the glass
door as it closed behind me,
in the porchlight the pear
tree looked more smug
than ever. "And now," she said,
as I perused the photos
on her fridge of mother and
son, "I make him do it just
like she did to me. Yes, I
make him pick up pears before
soccer, or else he can't
play. And you know, I feel so
bad about it, because I know
he hates it like I did." And
she smiled a worried frown
as if she had just sent her
son off to be a migrant farm
worker in the San Joaquin Valley.
"And you know when he was

little, he used to love to pick
up pears with me. And now..." she
trailed off. "Hey," I replied, "that's
how we learn responsibility." And
then I said, "But if it's been
such a thorn in your family's
side for so long, did you ever
consider cutting it down?" "Yes,
but I just couldn't do it," and
she bit her lower lip thoughtfully.
While watching, I imagined doing
the same. "Well, it's getting
late. I'd better leave you
to get your rest," I said, and
took one last plunge in her
ocean eyes before retracing
my path down blue steps and into
the yard. "Be careful of the pears,"
she cautioned, as I stepped on
one in the dark. And the pear
tree smirked and giggled so hard,
its leaves rustled in the
perfectly still night air.

Portrait of the Lady and the Rhinoceros

The arm-draped armor-
plated rhino in the picture
with you seemed mysteriously
melancholy. Nonetheless,
I have a feeling that your presence
causes spontaneous smiles
on all but the most
reticent of creatures. Perhaps his
trepidation that the moment could
not last overcame his momentary joy.
Even so formidable a beast, having
found your arm around him
in that pose, must have had
to work very hard to suppress
a delighted smile, shyness
notwithstanding. Had I been
there in his stead, I know that
would certainly have been the case.
And I have no horn on my nose,
and my skin is thin and smooth.

Proof

You're proving I don't love you,
like slippery rain
proves the ground, or December proves
an August decadence, or the
planting heart of a young
boy proves the threshing man.

But this is merely pudding proof,
slapped together in the heat of hunger,
flown fish-tailed from a fog bank,
a misty-eyed withdrawal mostly,
into the sun, into
the tampered sun, into the
purple, perfect passion
of the tampered sun.

There I go, catching insects with geodesic eyes,
casting saltines
on the humming wing, on
the fragile wing.
There I go.

Sew me wide-eyed to the fabric of
your tongue. I will navigate your
span of sighs to enter triumphant at the
Golden Gate, a firedrake's harbor inlet
for the Golden Hinde.

You must listen to hear the silence. I
will roar above roaring,
above the delicious, above
the fragments, above all.
But still torn
by your trembling, by
your wriggling out from
dreams, from sleepless dreams.

Pruning

Smiles she peddled were all aglistening,
miles more than simply glistening.
I'll slip on lips leagues nearer, as if listening.
Never tiring of her voice so rude,
ever sensual, naughty, gruff and crude,
verifying to the sticking point my courage screwed.
Draping silk on spider spotters,
raping vessels void of potters,
aping now the sleeker otters.
(But really to the)
tears in her eyes which, behind a glass of charm,
tear my heart along a dotted harm,
tea for two inside a canyoned arm.
(Now following her advice for pruning life I)
strew the platitude,
true the latitude,
rue the attitude.

Questions

"This may be a stupid question,"
she said, and ventured to ask an
intelligent question about my
work, not knowing me well at all,
our familiarity merely hours old. I
listened seemingly intent, while
hopelessly lost in her fathomless eyes,
climbing out occasionally with some
difficulty, if only to stay reasonably
connected to the conversation so as not to
appear a) indifferent b) inattentive or
c) hopelessly lost in her fathomless eyes. "This
may be a stupid question," she began again
some time later, asking a perceptive question
about another aspect of myself with which
she was understandably unfamiliar, while I
listened like a cobra to flute music, completely
bewitched by the sorcery of her smile, occasionally
breaking the spell with no little effort if only
to muster a barely adequate answer, not wishing to
seem a) distracted b) disinterested or c) completely
bewitched by the sorcery of her smile. "This may be
a stupid question," she began again later, and
continued with sagacity on a subject I now
remember nearly nothing about, because at
the time I was also playing a scene between
us in my mind. "This may be a stupid question,"
she would say in my little drama, lying
in my arms (after all it is my scene) by
a cobalt blue lake under star-flooded skies,
and then would proceed to pose one of her
typically insightful queries. "Come on," I would
reply, kissing her ripe mouth, "you'll have to do
better than that." "Why?" she would ask hesitatingly,
carefully stroking my hair, somewhat
taken aback by my evidently impending

criticism. "Because," I would say, teasing the top button of her blouse, "you've been promising one all evening, but so far, I haven't heard a stupid question yet."

Ragged Boy

Boy,
ragged boy,
I see you with shirttails
flapping in the wind,
in the April days
before, just before, the crocus
peeps its yellow head above the
snow-stained ground.
Ragged boy,
I count the holes in your
jangled jeans from a discreet distance
to fool the shame in the April days
during kite-flying flings.
Ragged boy,
gentle boy, you talk
to animals like prophets,
and spare the fat mosquito
its crab-shell fate,
while I, the designated mentor,
am wheel-barrowed
through the streets unconscious.
Tell me boy,
ragged boy,
how can I unlearn?
Where can I be driven
in a chamoised Chevrolet,
to begin again
to surrender to the lost in you,
my boy, my ragged child,
emperor of my boyhood,
brother born of beauty,
ragged boy?

Remnants

> *Today the only remnants of dodos once seen alive are a single decapitated head, some skins, fragmented bits of this and that, and a mismatched pair of feet. - NY Times*

Last night I bled a bit from my life
and dripped a little on my soul.

Today I ask you to share a foot,
because they need two to
make a final pair.
They'll never think of them as us,
you and I who once craved life like they,
now only ill-fitting pieces that elicit
stifled laughter from those
whose feet still match. Mother told me
I'd be special, but the last remnants
of a race erased was not what
she foresaw when her eyes cradled mine.

Come my darling,
since we cannot both the one head be,
put your last foot next to mine. For if
they are to have only two,
let them be
two that loved.

Ride

he downshifts into second
Those lines you
he downshifts into first
worry about,
he tells her engine idling
they're beautiful. They speak
revs the motor
to your courage.
he floors it
Those few extra pounds
squealing spinning tires
you agonize over,
car fishtails badly
never looked
he straightens her out
better on anyone. Those
pushing 75
years you worked, and earned,
pushing 100
and studied, and fought, and
pushing 130
loved, and hoped,
he chokes back the throttle
          and the tears
         yes the tears...
         car coasts to an idle
in light of present times were
he turns the ignition off
the formative years. You
he sets the parking brake
make it, but you get out shaking.

Rivers

By the evening river,
where the coffee-cup
ripples rehearse in tiny
chorus lines prancing
on wrinkled sunsets at
my feet, there we meet,
though you never
know. There with my
arms at my side, I embrace
you slowly, like the river's
arms embrace each bend,
each bar, each bank, in an
ever flowing, ever folding
motion, and yet, motionless.

Swim with me tonight,
sing the river's song. I'll race
through the years to finish
in your eyes. Stay with me
tomorrow for spring's first
dawn, when the sun's straw
rays sip the breathless water.
Let me brush the cobwebs
from your smile, and kiss
you where the river once
kissed you, and then
danced on.

Tonight meet me at the
river's edge. I'll wade
through galaxies and swim
the sun's eclipse to be by
your side. I'll brave the eye
of a solar storm and walk
its windless waves. Nothing
can keep me away if you

will meet me there, by a
river of comets on Neptune's
nether moon, dressed only
in a dwarf star's glittering
dust, and Orion's belt.
Wait for me on a blanket
of handspun Northern
Lights, bone warm beside
St. Elmo's fire. I'll be
wearing a red constellation.

Rose-Quilted Beds

Rose-quilted beds
have been my undoing.
It seems I always must
propose to a woman
I see sitting or lying
(God willing) on a
rose-quilted bed.
Imagine picking roses,
of all things, to put
on quilts, as if
quilt manufacturers
were real sentimentalists.
But quilts are cool, and
the reason that they
are cool is that they
are warm, like ovens
right out of your
muffin. Have you
tried Betty Crockpot's
muffins? She sells
them all over town.
Get your red-hots.
Get your red-hot rose
quilts. Have you ever
proposed to three
different women on
three successive nights?
My friend Jack did.
"Each one was so
beautiful, I just had
to propose." Now,
that doesn't sound
to me like he meant
clothed beauty. And
how unfortunate,
particularly if they

all accept. Do I detect
a rose-quilted bed
lurking in the shadows?
Rose-quilted beds, I'm
telling you, rose-quilted
beds will undo us all.

Rules for Life

Dearest children:

Now that I've gone, you've probably opened the envelope that said, "Open this when I'm gone." Otherwise you wouldn't be reading this, unless you are a snoop or a cat burglar or a tabloid reporter. Just wanted to leave you a list of things that I would hope would help you, since I'm not around to do it anymore. Wherever I am, you can be sure that I still love all of you (even if you can be aggravating at times). So now, on with the list. Words to live by from a dead man, that's ironic isn't it? Here goes:

Take out the trash.

Remember that nine out of ten times, people will disappoint you. But see every person you meet as the tenth person until they prove otherwise, and when they do, continue to see them as the tenth and maybe they'll catch on. To see everyone as the nine, is to miss the tenth entirely.

If you must live a Christian life, live the Beatitudes and not the Inquisition.

If you must live a Jewish life, live the children of Israel and not the state of Israel.

If you must live an Islamic life, let one of your inspirations be Muhammad Ali.

If you must live an exemplary life, let one of your inspirations be Gene McDaniels.

If you need to look up to people, walk around on your knees. This is preferable to actual hero worship, since the heroes are probably no better than you.

If you are a woman, have patience with the men, because they need lots of help.

If you are a man, have patience with the women, because they need lots of help.

Don't live life to the fullest. Live life to the half-fullest, and use the other half to reflect on how you can do better with what you have left of the first half.

The expressions of life are always changing, whether we want them to or not. Learn to find joy in the change, rather than sorrow in the passing. And if you can't find joy in the change, check the large bills, people say there is a lot of joy in those.

Your life is a rare and exclusive privilege. Treat it as such. But kick it in the butt every now and then, just to keep it honest.

Let the individuality of life remind you of the Creator. Every leaf, every snowflake, every blade of grass, every tiny speck of life is unique and different. It takes a caring Workman with a great deal of patience to fashion that kind of detailed beauty. We are a part of that work. We may get the feeling we're the ass-end of a donkey sculpture sometimes, but we are a fine work, nonetheless.

Beware of expecting too much from others and from oneself. Expect just enough. To do otherwise is to live a discouraged or discouraging life. Unless you want one of those, in which case we'll make fun of you and ostracize you from the family.

Find the humor in life and share it in laughter with others, unless they don't happen to find it funny, in which case have them shot. I mean, give them a shot… in the arm sort of thing… or of bourbon… you know…

Listen to your thoughts. Listen in silence, so you hear everything. Listen in earnest. Now listen in Poughkeepsie. If it sounds the same, dance to it cheek to cheek with whomsoever is closest.

Put the toilet paper roll on the toilet paper roll holder. How many times do I have to tell you?

Suspend fear with love, first for yourself, then for others. And if that doesn't work, suggest to the others that you may be willing to start a nuclear exchange, and that you just did.

Seek out all kinds of artists and artisans who revel in excellence: sculptors, singers, painters, actors, musicians, writers, engravers, glass blowers, silversmiths, potters and the like. Particularly dancers in tights, cause that way you can see what you sought.

Feel the Power that made you, that is you, consciously, at least once a day. Then thank yourself for it. If you don't believe in a Power, feel that instead. That'll make things a bit chillier, so just dress warmly.

Don't waste any of your life being angry. I have already wasted enough of it for all of us.

As a certain poet whose initials are DCJ and who looks a great deal like me said: "Get life under your fingernails so it never comes out, not with hand cleaner, not with nail files, not with death." And if you figure out what that means, let me know. After all, I'm the poet, I should know what the hell my poems mean, even if someone else has to tell me.

Life is a Canterbury Tale, rather than a Tale of Woe. Alternative version: Woe unto the Tail that gets its Berry caught in a Canter.

If I have managed anything of dignity, forgive me for it. And if I have perpetrated improprieties, thank me for them. Think not as others think. Remember, as the latest version of the Bible states, "Do what you want to do, go where you want to go." No wait, that was an early rock song. I always get those two so confused.

Get plenty of sleep. How many times do I have to tell you?

Look out for liars. You can always tell if someone is lying because they blink. At least, that's what I learned from social media. I think we should pattern our court system on that premise. Even the death penalty. The guy blinked, execute him. Hell, it's as good a system as we have now. And probably twice as accurate.

When people let you down, go somewhere out into Nature and open yourself wide to the Nature of life, except during snowstorms, hailstorms, avalanches, tornados, floods, hurricanes, heat waves, windstorms, duststorms, sleet, freezing rain, deluges, thunderstorms, lightning storms, thunder and lightning storms, nor'easterlies, tsunamis, volcanic eruptions, earthquakes, continental shifts, meteor showers, cataclysmic events, revolutions, locust storms, mosquito season, black fly season, black widow mating season, grizzly bears saying grace, and other inappropriate, inopportune or insolent times. Just wanted to be clear about that.

Remember the golden rule: do unto others as you would have others do unto you. If you can't remember the golden rule, remember the silver rule: do unto others, but wait until you see what they are going to do unto you, then answer in kind. If you can't remember the silver rule, remember the brass rule: shut up or I'm gonna have to smack you with this brass thing.

Violence is not the answer, unless of course you're talking about a pre-emptive strike, then it's okay 'cause that's what our government advocates. Casualties will be kept to a minimum. We reserve the right to set the minimum.

Take care of each other. This is very important. That's what families are for. That and family feuds, take your pick.

Count your blessings on your fingers. If you get past one hand, you are more fortunate than most people. Award yourself an additional blessing for being so blessed. Avoid stopping on the middle finger.

Clean your room. How many times do I have to tell you?

Did you take your vitamins?

Good night, love you, see you in the morning.

Your loving father,

Me

Sarah Radiant

Sarah, radiant in
blue jeans, arms
clasped behind her
head, tank top gently
but barely holding her,
letting her alabaster belly
escape, becomes
a painting Klimt would
have sacrificed all
others to create.
Her ivory necklace,
that might be nothing
more than glass, would
gladly be accepted in
trade for a Czar's crown
jewels, if only for the
pricelessness of having adorned,
for however brief an
instant, so immortal a throat.
Kim Novak in Bell, Book and
Candle would surely have
traded even Pywacket to
look half so entrancing. I am
neither a famous painter nor
a caretaker of Russian
treasure nor a movie star,
but I too would trade the
the most valuable thing I
might obtain, even the
bluest of moons, could I
reach it, to feel only
the merest of glances
from her subduing eyes.
Now where did I put that
extra tall celestial ladder?

Second Skin

Another pair of pants
are worn to strands, fabric for a
second skin, worn both thin
and tattered by my hasty pursuit
of life, without the realization that
life, in her infinite wisdom
and bare-kneed embroidery,
was pursuing me.

Session

Deep down the prairie alleyway
with the strange street name lies
the studio door disguised
as the petrified gates of a great battlefield,
an urban Little Big Horn in downtown Philly.
"Tell me what are you trying to find,"
she commands (as I clamber over icy hillocks
packed hard like women's broken hearts), a question
needing lifetimes to answer, but I flank the urge
to volley philosophically and instead give her
a more regulation answer – "Baker Sound
I have a session..." "Follow me,"
she orders imperiously as Custer must have,
and I the horseless seventh cavalry
follow, facing not a skirmish against sharp-nosed arrows
but against sharp-eared microphones listening like birds
before a thunderstorm. I lose less
than Armstrong's horse soldiers,
merely my voice caged for a price,
a disembodied prisoner of war
repeating only name and rank, retreating to the corner
of 17th and Market.
I still have my voice in much the same way a trooper's wife
still has her tears long after the battle with no survivors.
What is missing is measurable only on a scale
of golden-haired generals
who underestimate the strength of the opposition.

Shootout

She filled her
torn-at-the-knees-but-beautifully-patched-
here-and-there-but-especially-there jeans
like a gunfighter fills his hand,
cool and killer from the front,
awe-inspiring from the back.
In a contest of wills she was
William Bonnie and I was William
Tell, although I never would
(tell that is). I
wanted to disarm her and
take her into my custody,
no lawman I, not even vigilante,
only a concerned citizen,
an insolent bystander
with a desire, oh yes,
to see justice done, if she is justice,
and to do her myself.
Oh, that I were her hands, that
I might slip behind her cartridge belt,
and squeeze her gun butt, and
cock her revolver.
She was so good I wanted to
shoot questions and ask first later,
although I had no questions,
so I held my fire with my finger itchy-trigger.
"How many notches on her gun?" I wondered.
I wanted only hers on mine
(gun that is),
and a big one
(the notch I mean).
So she drew on me and grew on me,
and I grew on her and drew,
and when the smoke cleared,
we both lay sprawled
in the street

(if beds are streets).
I listened for her breathing.
Oh, how she was breathing.
I looked for wounds,
she had none. I
looked again and looked,
and again I looked, just in case.
We both were fine,
though I had taken one in the heart.
Now she fills my
torn-at-the-knees-but-beautifully-patched-
here-and-there-but-especially-there dreams
like a gunfighter fills his whiskey glass,
over and over
and over.

Snowing

Pandering for snow,
pan piping outside my mental bungalow,
panning slow,
straining to see
first flake, the very first
flake to fall
from cloud jaws hovering,
hungering to be slavering in snow…
I lost my train of thought.
No matter, an express comes in
every half life,
one now from California
from two places where I grew sideways,
forever over and beyond,
knowing and grown until
sabled. Sixty-four new winters say
resplendence at thirty and two is ivory asymmetry.
Anticipate at sixty-four and more the kingdom of the my,
and you ask why,
and never ask why.

So I'm Coming Around a Corner

So I'm coming around a corner
on 103 between Kittery Point
and York, a stretch of road just
inland from the beach where
there are no visible houses, but
guarded on the left side by railing
and hills going up on the right,
and it's just getting to be dusk,
and this car is slowly backing out
of a driveway down one of
those hills out from the trees,
and as I make the
corner I see this car backing into
my path about a hundred yards
ahead, and as I try to stop,
the sudden patches of snow left
on the road from the small storm
last night catch my wheels and they
start to skid, and whereas ordinarily
I would be able to stop, the patches
toy with me like an invisible
hand and the car keeps backing
out, and I have to let up on the brakes
to end the skid and I lean on my horn
and the car still keeps backing out
and I'm not going any slower,
but I am running out of road
as the car still keeps backing out
over the center line now, and
I'm running out of road and
I try the brakes again but my wheels
slide again and I keep laying
on the horn and it all seems to grow
very still… and I am left no room
and I'm still laying on the horn
but silently now, as he keeps backing out,

and I manage to squeeze, I don't know
how, between the car and the guard rail,
flying by at forty-five, and
as suddenly as I was on him
I am passed him, and I'm too
surprised to swear, and who
knows what that guy was thinking
or if it was a guy, it was too dusky
to tell. But I can tell you this, that was
a damn close miss, and I expected
to hear crunching metal at any second,
but didn't,
as if a major life change, within a span
of seconds, was both introduced
and then voted down by the universe
at the last possible moment.

Song for the Children

Please put down your toys and listen
to what your father has to say.
You're the handsomest bunch of boys and girls,
but your mother has gone away.

She said to tell you she loves you,
each and every day,
then she opened the door late last night,
while you all were tucked away,

and she kissed me goodbye forever,
and said, "Take care of my babies please."
Then she walked out the door and disappeared,
and left all of you here with me.

We'll still call ourselves a family,
even though your mother's gone,
and you know I'll never leave you,
and without her we'll carry on.

For we still have each other,
and it will always be that way.
You're the handsomest bunch of boys and girls,
but your mother has gone away.

Sonnet Odyssey

The woman grows despite the claustral climes,
beleaguered still by gnomic ghosts of when,
as reaching for contemporary rhymes
spills awkwardly the puerile poet's pen.
The valiant verse with time will sweet mature
to chant a mythologic siren's song,
whose sharper syntax severs sailor's cure
from lyric lashed to broken mast too long.
The paradox resolves with fabled sense
in time upon enchanted elder roads,
where simile duality repents,
like diamond hungry sisters spitting toads.
In odysseys, the darker is the day,
the brighter shines the star that lights the way.

Spooncatcher

The wind bit fiercely
at our sandwiches and
onion rings, and yanked
our hair at odd angles. I
tried to take the sports cap
off of
a new bottle of water, but I
couldn't turn it easily, and
wouldn't turn it too hard
for fear of breaking it.
"Been working out much?" she
asked with a smile, as I put a half-
nelson on the plastic top. "Yes,
and I'm going to try punching
my way out of a paper bag next," I
responded, and caught her
spoon as it blew by. "Nice
catch," she said, thereby
immortalizing me in the
only important
Spooncatcher Hall of Fame.

Startled

Meekly,
eyes peeled, I
left her apartment house, looking right and left
for signs of someone watching me, watching for
her. When, as if on cue, she drove her
grey four-door into the dust-gray
parking lot, and quickly parking,
out she jumped, busying herself no doubt
with accouterments, and never noticing me standing with
my hands in my
side pockets, trying to decide
whether to approach her or whether
to wait for her to
see me first. And while I was deciding, the ecstasy
of choice ceased to be mine, as she sort of
looked through me, then looked
at me, her breath at
odds with her throat, her voice just odd,
betraying little of what was to be,
no disdain, yet no
damsel joy. "Damn,
you startled me," she said. "Me?" I asked. "Yes, you!"
Me? Somehow now the friendly fiend? Somehow me,
the gregarious ghoul, the
kindly kong? "I miss you," I said, and kindly
she did not respond directly. But she
asked about the boys. "They're men unmasked,
growing up," I said, and said it in a way as if growing
into manhood were an alleviation of the serious condition
of childhood. "One has moved out of
the house. The
one's (the middle one's) voice is changing. Only one
is still a boy. The other is
man, or half-man,
or centaur, or
satyr," I joked. And still she stood blasé,

with purse, with bags, with
drawing paper book in hand, neither withdrawing
nor advancing, but firmly trying to ignore.
"Yes, I'm in a hurry and yes,
I, oh, look at the time, must go now." And so she went. While I
(mind you well) polited my
way through the parting, never being offended or turning away
(toujours la politesse), never asking why, when she was too
busy arriving, that suddenly she needed to be too busy
leaving. And yet I know, and sadly I believe,
still tonight in thoughts of crystal,
she lingers lovely in her purple flowered dress. "You startled me," she
again recites, as I replay the scene on eyelids yet again,
fighting for the why of everything and losing the fight,
over and over.
"You startled me," she says. "You
startled me. Damn, you startled
me."

Stieglitz You and I

The carriages have long ago clattered past...
Forever alone, caught in mid-step, the girl in the street
and her hemmed shadow, severed momentarily from
one raised foot, have long since abandoned
the destination of their walk and
an earthly nineteen eleven France, for the less than
perfect ones living now only in our minds...
We watch her cryogenically
through Stieglitz boxed eye, and can
still sail for rainy Paris on the morrow
having wasted more than a century since
he was there, waiting for us on the dock,
ignorant yet of Georgia and all we have to
say to him of portraits and equivalents... And
afterwards, we will take our own photographs
in scented rooms, and cross dozens
of shiny streets while carriages clatter past,
until we too are caught mid-stepping through eternity
in blacks and grays, but together...

Stuffed Animal Crisis

The little voice was going to bed when
the cry went up for Boofer Dog,
and we searched the house
low and high,
under calico couches and
behind beige chairs.
We looked outside the van,
inside the toy box,
and even knocked on Auntie's
door to make certain
he wasn't hiding in there
while she was sleeping.
"Boofer Dog!" said the little voice
now more concerned than ever,
and the search intensified,
with flashlights and teams
turning everything topsy-turvy.

But Boofer Dog
had decided to take
the night off, and
remain at Grandma's
to be picked up the next day.
Informed of this,
the little voice seemed content
to wait and sleep
with only one last murmur
for the recalcitrant,
but beloved,
Boofer Dog.

Stupid Poem

he took off his hand
and placed it on her leg
he took off his leg and
placed it in her hand
he took off his stomach
and laid it on her breast
he took off his head
but his only hand
slipped and his head
bounced off the ground
and hit her knee
and his eyes slid
down her dress but
his lips caught her hem
and with the help of
a strong tongue pulled
his mind and all
attached features
home to her lap as
he muttered
something about
going to pieces
every time they
make love

Submission

Here goes —
this could be my shot at
getting included in the Best American
Poetry 2022. (We have published poems by God.)
Let's see how to approach it — humorous? No, considered
too skinny. Confessional? No, what
is there left (Reports in two lifetimes or less.)
to say that Sexton didn't back then,
unless it would be ejaculation
at forty instead of menstruation? I
know, I'll shoot for the inobvious
stated in a routinely subliminal,
yet vaguely stilted way. Free verse of course — no every
body does that. (Pays two old copies of
TV Guide.) Perhaps if I knew
who the editor would be, I could
tailor my style to her/his tastes. But
what would those be? Did he/she
she/he tee/hee learn life leafing through books,
youth buried in stacks — a bomb-
shelter junkie waiting, still waiting
for the big bad boom? (Simultaneous submissions okay, but
will be burned.) Or was her/his,
her, I tell you, her life lived among
the urban cannabis, smoking their
faces in a fine haze, or drinking
their own blistered blood from frosty mugs,
vampires of Savannah T&A? (It is indeed our lack of concern
and compassion, as well as our over-inflated sense of self-worth,
that make rejections seem so cold and impersonal.)
But screw all that. I really don't need their
acceptance. Did Roethke, did Dickinson,
did cummings, love that Bob, did
Jonson, my idols, my golden calves,
mooing from the pages, from the
gritty, crumbling pages, (Brief cover letter of

less than one word is good.)
gone now to that poetry barn in the sky, to
be milked by the divine hand that
untimely ripped the birth sack (Be yourself or anyone else.)
from their twisted eyes in the pilot of All
Poets Great and Slimy? But
I digress, digest, infest, beau geste,
bovine, full circle. (Don't let the discouragement
of rejection discourage you, you reject.) Leave me now,
I must compose. Fraught with hangers-
on, I must divest and deshirt and
deplane. (We are a very arrogant market to break
into.) This is my shot — reload, ramrod, powder,
ball and patch, red laser-spot on forehead,
squeeze the pen, don't pull it.
But really — who reads that crap anyway?
(We have published some of the most disingenuous poetry
in American literature.) Leave me now, I am in da Nile,
Da Vinci, duh. Leave me now, I must bemoan my
fatalism. I vant to be unknown. (More poems received than
there are people in some galaxies.)
Leave me now,
I must create...

Synchronicity

We had this discussion
ten years ago, I think,
when you had definitely
piqued my interest. But
at the time, you were put
off by your recent
disappointments with men,
and I being a man,
was just another
potential disappointment.

Now, ten years later,
again you have definitely
pinnacled my interest. But
again this time, you are put
off by your recent
disappointments with men,
and I, being still a man,
am still just another potential
disappointment.

I feel like tungsten,
waiting patiently in
line to be discovered
in experiment one thousand
and one, only to find
that Edison has given
up at experiment
one thousand.

We could have made
beautiful light bulbs together.

Tears for Luke

I should have taken him,
but who can see down
long roads past future bends,
and who could imagine heroin
and crack and arrests and
rehabs and relapses and
flights from authorities
and phone calls asking for
money for a bus ticket
to shoplift in yet another town
and be arrested yet again?
"If I kill myself, will
you take Luke?" she asked
when he was only three months
old. But I already had two of
her children to raise and Luke
wasn't mine. Still, I should have
taken him. I should have never
let him slip through my fingers,
though it was hard to keep much
of anything from slipping
through except the children.
When I brought his
brother and sister to visit their
mom I remember little
Luke being cut and
scratched and having a
lump on his head. He fell,
she said, and I didn't doubt it.
I should have taken him then,
instead of his grandparents,
who did the best they could,
but not as good as the three
of us might have done.
And now his brother and sister
would only have to be worrying

about what college he should
get his graduate degree from, or
which job he should take,
instead of what jail he is in
tonight, and if he will ever
straighten himself out, and if
he will even live to reach thirty.

Test

She was nineteen and my friend's
lady, and I was the friend needing
work, given the job of painting the
ceiling of the Lake Arrowhead A-frame.
She and I had seen each other several
times before, but never without Neal,
while Neal and I had shared the
same ladies before, but not at the same
time. Sometimes I was second, but that
was delicious, I admired his tastes. So,
on this almost innocent day, I climbed
the two hundred feet of wooden stairs
to their cliffside cabin, and met him
just going out on errands. He stayed, and
talked amenities, and about what he wanted
done with blue paint over rough wood.
Then he excused himself for the
errands, closing the door without
a backward glance. The and-one-and-two
rhythm of his feet falling to faint,
subsided to my looking over the job at
hand. She and I talked for a minute, then
she dropped this –
"I can't believe Neal was stupid
enough to leave me alone with you."
– stunning thing!
Excuse me, did I really just hear that
from this Venus named Michelle? But
one kiss creamed all doubt, and she
retired unattired to the little guest
bedroom overlooking the front porch
and the solid swinging gate that blocked
the view of the two hundred feet of
panting steps. "I can't," I said, and
still to this day I don't know if
it was the desire for comity or fear

of being caught, though I wasn't afraid
of Neal. And so I returned to painting
the unconsummated ceiling, every
rough plank her soft skin.
I never saw either of them again after that.
Maybe it was one grand selfless act. Maybe
it was not wanting to mix fear and love.
Maybe it was knowing what it feels like
to be hurt and not wanting to hurt. "Good!"
said my large friend with the five children
who had strong moral fundamentalist leanings.
"Good for you!" he said, and smiled, not
knowing I had failed the same test
with his wife just a month earlier.

The Assembly

"Did you ever see a bear coming
and climb a tree?" Buffalo Bill
asked in front of four hundred
second graders one New York day. (Is
the word Albany related to the
word albino? Probably not.) She (Annie
Oakley) brought her own hat but wore
mine, or the one that my
friend's wife gave me after their split-
up. And do I remember our
songs that flowed in and out of arroyos
in an inn, famous flat out
for touting its comfort
(says so right in the
name)? Oh, do I! Later
she refused and thanked me,
an odd combination. But, thankfully, I
refused to be refused,
and then she thanked me
again. (Doesn't the odor
of interstate rest stops smell like that of
a grimy hospital?) I
love the road, and Annie's star, and the laughter of
the cherished of 400 families. And so what if
the photographs weren't very clear? We still have
the chemicals in our brains to
remind us. "No, but I saw a tree coming once
and climbed a bear," I tossed
back to Buffalo Bill in my best
unspecified drawl. She brought
her own heart but wore mine.

The Ballerina and the Clown

All day long the clown
sat wondering about
the ballerina, and if one
who danced so gracefully
could ever truly love
one who stumbled so
laughingly. Then there was
his big red nose, whereas
hers was petite and, well,
nose-colored. And so
he pondered, and night
encroached, and too
the hour of their
meeting. Finally
he arose and dressed
himself in a larger
version of her tutu,
thinking to himself the heart
of a clown could do
no less for love. Attired
in this, he pirouetted clumsily
on tiptoe to the appointed
spot, just as a fiery darkness
slipped its orange
veil across the sun's
nervous glance. She
came from out of nowhere
and floated and
stood a few feet away, as
eyes drank in eyes.
Then a smile sprinkled the
clown's grin-drenched
face, but a real smile, and
a tear waterfalled to his heart.
He placed a careful kiss
under the canopy

of two big red noses. She
had dressed as a clown.

The Chickadee

In the wings of my mind,
I had already picked up
a hundred times
the dead chickadee
that had caused her to
utter an audible sigh
when first she saw it through
the sliding glass door, the
poor bird lying
on the porch in a little
heap as if struck like
Apollo's son from the sky
in the middle of flight.
I had thought about whether
to wear trepidacious gloves,
and how to pick
the helpless shell of
the departed avian up
by its tail feathers hoping
they would not pull out. But
I don't like touching dead
things. It seems, just like
the uncurtained windows
of the NY hotel that night
thirty-five floors up and
tilting, they want to suck
out life, being but a vacuum
of life now themselves.
I thought about the
wood-handled shovel which
I would need anyway
to institute a proper burial.
But, especially now that the
passing of this bird had
been consecrated by her pity,
a shovel or gloves were not

suited and only bare fingers
in a final caress on its sad
little form would suit the
solemnity of the occasion.
And so overnight I prepared
myself, and in the morning
began the wake walk
to the porch. But when I
looked out the sliding glass
door, the chickadee
was gone. I can only hope,
for her pity's sake, that it
revived and flew away, rather
than being absconded
with by some burglar cat
late that night while I,
the Hamlet in this tragedy
of a chickadee, pondered.

The Day He Quit

It wasn't too long ago he wanted to be
in the NBA, he loved basketball so much.
Years full of days he spent beneath
our neighbor's basket, putting the ball up.
Back in again. Back in again. Back in again.
Keeping it from their dog. But today
he quit the high school basketball team.
And he's not sad, he's happy. It wasn't
that he wasn't playing, he was. For
the first time in his life, he was playing
all the time, quick hands on defense,
leading in assists, passing up shots to
feed the ball inside, freezing defenders
with his angular drives. And it wasn't that
they weren't winning, even though
they weren't. Nothing could be as
bad as that winless season two years
ago at the other school. But the fun
had gone out of it. A surly coach,
blaming the team for not living
up to his responsibility, for not winning
with his system, for not making him look
good. Back in again. Back in again.
Years full of days. And he's not sad, he's
happy. I'm the one who's sad. Never to see
him play high school basketball again. I had
no time to prepare myself. The season had six
more weeks, six more weeks now without
him. No time to prepare. It wasn't too long
ago he wanted to be in the NBA. I smiled a
parent's knowing smile and said, "If that's
what you want, I know you can do it. But
it's not easy." Years full of days. Back
in again. Back in again. But he's not
sad. Today he quit the high school
basketball team, but he's not sad.

Back in again. Back in again.
Years full of days. He's happy.
I'm the one who's sad.

The Gallery

Stepping through her apartment door
I emerged into a Vermeer,
the painter's studio,
a 17th century entrance into clarity of form and line,
the play of light between floor and fabric,
the warmth of Dutch color.

While confiding in conversation
she reclined to become
a living David portrait,
my very own Madame Recamier,
the quintessence of woman
clothed in empyrean elegance,
born of divine brush strokes
and a god's imagination.

Her vividness was my personal Gauguin,
my Tahitian woman with sunflower
in the midnight tropics of
her living room.

And now,
having studied in her world,
no longer do I require
the masters of Amsterdam or Paris or Tahiti.
For I am Rembrandt, and
she is my self-portrait. I
am Da Vinci,
and she is my sketchbook.
I am Michelangelo,
and it is she I reveal upon the ceiling,
she I discover within the stone.

The Great Canola Oil Controversy

They say, don't touch it!
One drop accidentally spilled
on the skin is enough to
kill a man! (And to think
I fried my dinner in it last
night. Good thing I fed
most of it to the cat. Speaking
of which, where is the cat?)
And imagine what it has done to
the land! Since it comes from
rapeseed, what do you expect?

Don't believe a word of it!
the Others say, it's Urban Legend!
(But I don't live in Urba. I don't
even know where Urba is. Yahoo
Maps doesn't even know. Maybe
they mean urbane. Urbane legend.
Now I can identify with that!) Hear me,
oh ye of little taste!
The gospel natural food truth
is: canola oil will bring
sight to the blind, hearing
to the deaf, and wisdom
to the unenlightened!
Oh, my brothers and sisters,
it will scrub your floors,
and paint your fence,
and do your nails,
and nail your dos,
and turn your don'ts into
why-the-hell nots! But don't
believe me. Just take a look
at my documentation. This
organization, this society,
this association, this scientific

body, this dual-carbed personality
says I'm right. It's good
enough to bathe in, drink
even! Matter of fact, I
drank some just a minute ago
and boy did it go
down smooth!

It is the devil incarnate! They
say, and make the sign of the
safflower. A better oil, a more
standard oil, would be oil
from a real plant, because
it has been recently verified that
canola oil, gasp, comes from…
oh my dear God in heaven…
a CAN! Can you
believe it? They make it from re-
processed cans! That's why
they call it CANola oil, Einstein!
No wonder they told us it was low
in fat. It's low in everything
but steel! It's even got low
self-esteem, but then,
esteem power went out
with the esteem-powered
locomotive. And speaking
of loco motives, listen to Them!
They're probably on the payroll
of the canola companies. And
we've recently heard that workers
have been killed in canola plants,
and they just throw them
into the vats and mix them
in with the rest of the oil.

Bullpucky! the Others say,
gesturing emphatically.

How dare you uninformed
people be so uninformed!
And I say unto you, inform
yourselves! And they again
list their official canola
truths, oily fingers
tapping on greasy palms.

(Meanwhile, I think
I'll have a salad for
breakfast, *without*
dressing. But then,
I never dress for
breakfast.)

The Ground Eaters

I just read about
how some slaves in
early America
would eat earth,
ordinary earth,
in order to kill
themselves, rather
than live as a
slave, gradually,
over months, wasting
away to decrepitude
and dizzying decay.
They were called
ground eaters, and
had not the finesse
of the tongue-swallowers
to suffocate themselves,
nor the glory of the
conflagration flagrants
to die by fire while
making not a sound,
nor the efficiency of
a true poison. Only
ordinary earth. Mother
earth. Only swallow her
day after day,
with a little water
and my daughter's
tearful attention
to how thin I've
become, and
how ashen.

The Kid Plays Hearts

Mummy told me if
I didn't take cards in
this game, I would win.
Instead, after being hit
with two moon hands in
a row and not taking a
card both times, I'm
getting my little butt
booted all over the place.
Mummy, you liar!

The Kiss

"Let's pose a painting
together, you and me,"
I suggested, and she
looked at me sideways
and said, "No I don't
think so, but nice
try though." And I
smiled. "I want to pose
a painting with you," I
said again a week or
so later, "I want to pose
Klimt's The Kiss, which
I knew was one of her
favorite paintings. But
she shook her head and
said, "No, it's too intimate."
And I understood why
she said it, the two of
us being only friends,
albeit very, very good
friends, and one of us
being attached elsewhere.
So I smiled once more,
because she always makes
me smile, and then I said,
"You're an actor. You
are more intimate onstage
in a Feydeau bedroom
farce than you will be
posing this painting. Why,
they don't even really
kiss." "That's true," she said,
still somewhat unconvinced.
"Besides," I said, "we're
already sitting on the
bed, and this is where I

was going to pose it."
So I gently took her hand
and lifted her up to her
knees. Then standing
on my knees near the
edge, I tenderly pulled
her accelerating heart
to mine, and for the first
time I felt her every curve
all at once, up and down
my being, dancing, even in
stillness, to the drumming
of our hearts. "They
don't even really kiss in
the painting," I repeated,
my voice trembling,
and I pretended to
consult a calendar of
Klimt's works in my right
hand open to February
and "The Kiss." But her hot
closeness made my eyes
fog. Then I decided
I had better uses for my
right hand anyway, and
put the calendar on
the floor and my hand
on her cheek, a cheek
infinitely more lovely
than the entire painting
itself. Then she placed her
hand over mine from the
inside, like in the painting,
and then I ask her to tilt
her head a little farther
to the left. Then I
placed my mouth very
close to hers, like in

the painting, and I struggled against an overwhelming urge to really kiss her. I felt her breath catch, and our hearts race together, probably like in the painting. "It's too intimate," she said and stepped off the bed, not like in the painting, pointing a finger at me from behind a broad smile. "How did you get me to do that?" she said, "Oh you're good!" And I smiled back, because she always makes me smile. "It's hard enough to stay away from you anyway," she continued, "without doing things like that." Then she said, "Let's go for a walk." And I agreed, although I can safely say that it was the furthest thing from my mind at the time, which was probably why she chose it. "Thank you," I said, as we walked to the door and stopped and turned face-to-face once again, but now a little farther away. "Thank you for putting aside your apprehensions and doing the pose with me." "Thank you too, it was fun," she confessed wryly. And I couldn't help but smile, because she always makes me smile.

The Last Bale

The point from appointed discussions having issued,
an iron glare clawed from the ardent garden rake we used.
The dastard time clock clucked verdant waves for vapid being,
forcing even loquacious aquatic lovers to acquiesce and cringe.

I had scarcely walked adored fields adorned by marigolds,
before the earth, fingered between their wretched roots, was sold.
Outdistancing, while they swathed gardens in a fluttering crosshatch,
I abandoned the singing of petals for a Mercury's snarling tach.

Pointless is three withered stalks on a weathered three-legged table.
So we savored the green grass growing on, God help us, the last bale.

The Last Days of PomPom

It was a sarsaparilla and whiskey-
flavored milkshake of a night
at Southern Amberhill University,
and the studied breathing of
some two thousand odd dreamy
educatees contrasted sharply
with the glare of a moon so white
it could only have come from the
udder of some galaxial bovine, while,
simply put, a fiend of unequal
proportions, unbeknownst to
all, preyed devoutly on an
unsuspecting few who would soon
pay the ultimate price, discounted
not a whit, for the evil, blooded,
louse-ridden, side-saddled deeds
of the many, or so it would seem,
only minutes from now, to Hetty
Button, bright-eyed co-ed of dorm
247, known throughout the campus
as 24/7 Hetty, but not to her friends,
far and few between though they
were, as the night continued to be
thrown, cross-seamed and fast-balled
over the outside corner of an eerily
proverbial, and umpireless, plate…
THUNK!

The Liberation

The President looked down
at the papers in front of him
then up with a faintly sardonic
grin playing on his face. "The
outcome however, is certain.
America will prevail." And
millions of Americans
applauded and beamed.

The little boy's lower leg dangled
precariously by a single tendon,
and he shuddered and moaned to
a world only he could know. His
once soft brown eyes caked with
blood, begged blindly for a
mother, or at least for a merciful god.

"We take seriously our mission
to liberate these people, and we
shall not be deterred until the
evil regime is ended and peace
is secured for all the world."

The pregnant woman had been
blown to pieces when the smart
bomb exploded, and the blast-born
fetus lay beside the parts that
had been her mother, a tiny
foot that never took a step,
twisted backwards and torn.

The Massage

"I'm so sore," she
moaned and I felt
bad for her karate-
bruised body, but
glad for her learning
experiences. "I need
a massage," she
intoned in a manner
that made me wish
I owned seven-league
boots, or had grown
two-hundred-
mile-long arms, or
knew a friend with
wings and an
afterburner. "I have
to go to sleep," she
murmured, and then
added, "I can't believe
I'm saying that, knowing
that there is a person
who has offered me
a deep muscle massage
and I'm not taking
him up on it." And we
both sighed into our
respective ends of the
phone, but I think I
sighed deeper. "Our
time will come," I
offered, as if patience
was at my fingertips,
while in my mind's eye
I had already begun
finger-strengthening
exercises, and chosen

a particularly sinful
body oil, and started
counting the nano
seconds and stacking them
in rows on my back porch
under a reassuring
"Tempus Fugit" sign.

The Orchard

We talked about a
picnic in the orchard
after Mark Twain's house,
but never quite got there.
She belongs in the house.
It should be hers, or one
as beautiful.

We looked for the orchard,
but settled, because of time,
for grassy banks beside a shy
stream hiding in rushes from
her course-changing smile.

Having forgotten a blanket
to sit on, we sat on apple crates
and used our laps for
tables. I put a corkscrew
to the wine, and poured
its bottled French sunlight
into makeshift plastic glasses.

She held her glass up to
toast, and I offered one
to picnics, but really meant it
to Bordeaux lips and
bewildering eyes.

The sun drank in as much
as we, and I know he was
peeved that she didn't
offer him part of her mozzarella
and tomato sandwich like she
did me. And of course,
my artichoke salad
went untouched.

The Tarriance

Chancely,
forgathered in the
mirkshade verdancy
of the forgrown,
I twired her raven elf locks
like a yuly fangle,
without a whingle,
without a whuffle,
rooven to her reddened lips
in a sweeting sweven,
umbethought of none
but her.

Thoughts

In the snow
I think of you,
below the feathered flakes pristine
I dream a world of crystalline,
that soars unseen for heaven bound,
then floats between, beneath and down...

In the sun
I think of you,
under saffron strands and gold
I dream of treasure yet to hold,
that shines so bold within a smile,
a flashing, flaming, flooding smile...

In the wind
I think of you,
inside a fleeing, flying gust
I dream of skies that slowly rust,
through swirling dust and zephyr doubt,
again with you, again without...

In the night
I think of you,
beside the brilliant, brittle moon
I dream of love that heals the wound,
that lights the tomb where lovers lie,
that touches you, that touches I...

In the rain
I think of you,
behind the weeping windows closed
I dream a flower no one knows,
that shames the rose and all things true,
now I give the flower to you.

Thoughts on a cool summers eve in April

if God were present in this room
even now he would be re-creating
the galaxies to mirror your face

(things(
life is a sled ride down an ever
steepening hill at first it's a curious
thing to be watching it all
moving then as years pass the sled
picks up speed things whir by at
heart-breaking speeds you can't get
off or turn it around and you
are alone on it and so it seems that all
there remains to do is fashion things(
dignity, art, a whittled stick(
to toss out along the way
to let the people who come
after us know that we were
here even as they…

have you ever done this 9you know
what I mean0? Forgot to push the
shift key when typing a parenthetical
statement 9what a dumbfug0

I don't mind compromising but
I will not be compromised

the fecund night air streaked
her tears with incessant fingers
while the moon bounced
incorporeal golden
boulders through the delicate
avalanche that is her hair

To a Former Valentine

Happy Valentine evening!
The dew is on the pumpkin,
and the hay is in the barn.
No wait, that's in the fall.
The snow is on heather,
and so is Billy.
No, that's silly.
The moon is in the corn,
and the corn is in the sink
being washed for supper. No
that's not it. Let's see, the
bloom is on the rose, and
the stuff is in the attic, and
everything one could ever
know is better known
by candlelight. From the
corner of Absentia and First,
from the citric depths
of a psychic orange grove,
I ask you, like a box of
chocolates says "Eat me,"
to light a taper or two, and
kindle a memory of we,
and blow a noisemaker for me.

Two Valentine Limericks

I

A vegetarian lady named Shockaly
found the road to romance rather rockily,
so each Valentine's day
she made sweet-toothed lovers pay,
by giving them hearts filled with broccoli.

II

A cheeky young cherub named Danny
fell in love with his friend Manny's Fannie,
one Valentine Dan
gave his lover a fan,
now Fannie sans Manny fans Danny.

Undazzled

Undazzled when we met, I
touched no roses in her smile, and
tasted not the sweetness of a summer
sky in the blueness of her eyes.

Bewildered by the bright, now I
dance in rose gardens garland
strewn, and dine deliciously on
endless azure feasts.

Unfortunato's Lament

You pompous old jackass Montressor,
Your head is just one big eraser.
Masonry is an art,
Not the way friends should part,
Think of poor Lady Fort, how'll you face her?

Who cares if Amonti or sherry,
If beavers be hirsute (that's hairy).
Let's drink to the truth
That your gin wants vermouth,
But I don't want you 'cause you're scary.

So go suck on a nugget of nitre.
If a vampire walks by go and bite her.
I'll see you next world,
Where the gates are all pearled,
Or in hell's breakfast nook, if it's righter.

Visually Arresting

My dear you are so… visually
arresting. I was visually arrested
once. Then I was blindly arraigned
at the Tactile County Courthouse.
It was a touching ceremony.
The arraign poured down. The
President of the Olfactory
Workers Union testified against
me. We went nose hair to nose
harem until I got a good wifery of him
and they separated us. Our
divorce is now pending, pending
a tail on a donkey, no questions assed.
Gus Tatory was my At Torney.
He had no taste for the proceedings
so he moved for dismissal but the
rest of the class was already gone.
They went to hear the Rubber Band
at Auditory Hall, a distant cousin
of Albert Hall, who was once married
to Annie Hall, but she expired and they
halled her away. Hall and Oates sang
the Dirge. Then the Dirge sang Forever
Young by Dylan until Neil Young
objected but the objection was
over-drooled on account of his youth.
When I went outside to feed my horses
hay and oats, they whinnied and
pawed the ground with their hooves,
spelling out: "Call me Ishmael," but
they left no number. The twelve million
monkeys on those keyboards over there
are still trying to catch up. So far the
most brilliant thing they have written is
"WEOOBMBMWEoooOverT;8sep97
REGtellmewhyP QrsTuVWxyKsSm

YaaSs1000DRS 999Ye=mccaWber8pt9
drinktomeonlywiththineaabercrobhnt9
dweebusyyoufdp9aardvarkEF9U-AP[ETHYL
5.P-KN95P-K5KGBCIAsameTHNG9e7
sleepitoffr=q]-305yo-h]pIt was the best
of times it was the worst of 4[0thj'
orig'awrj'pW."They scratch their
butts while typing, so the keyboards
are now unfit for human use. For-
tunately they are only outdated models.
I outdated a model once. She was
trained like a queen. We went to
Sausalito for sausage and hot sauce
and she walked like she was wearing one.
Actually she wore a b-shirt with Lost
and Won on the front. We were on
the lam, until it bleated mary had a little
and gave us away. A little known
chain of chain stores bought the rights
but they were only long brown rites
and not the Big Ben fluffy kind.
Then I woke down, got down and damn
near drowned for I was sleeping
on a boat at the time. It was a
trawler and spoke with a southern trawl,
but I got disused to it, and now am
sending this to you for your
apprusal, I mean peroval, I mean
move over monkeys and let
homo sapiens in on the task. To which
they replied, "We thought you'd
never task," so I didn't.
Yours in perspicacity… I mean,
polysyllabically… that is, in perpetuity.
Signed, liver boy, ah… livid buy, er
lover buoy… um…
me.

Watching Her Sleep

> *Busy old fool, unruly sun,*
> *Why dost thou thus,*
> *Through windows, and through curtains call on us?*
> *—John Donne*

Sleeve of night,
cuff of moon,
bluer than cold
hands, slide the
shade farther
down to
keep the sun
from intruding,
and let my lady
slumber so
I will have more
of the impudent
morning
to gaze at her,
like seeing an orchid blossom,
like sailing on a sea of glass,
like watching from behind a waterfall,
like riding circles on spotted hawk wings,
like tasting wild strawberries in puddles of cream.

Were the Woman I

Were the woman I
love only a tiny grain of
sand on the shores of a
stygian sea in some far-off
world, still would her eyes
shine so brightly,
that shadowy sailors on that
sea would daily thank their
equivalent of Neptune
for such a brilliant beacon
to steer by.

And the Maker of Worlds, some
where on the outer edges of
the universe still laying
down brick, would pause in his
infinite remodeling and stare
into the basement where
he thinks he left
the light on.

What if doctors traded places with carnival barkers?

Hey, get your procedure here! Come on, come on now!
You there, didn't you feel a little twinge when you
woke up this morning? We can fix that for you!
We can chase it out, cut it out, pray it out, burn it out,
treat it out, feel it out, make it right, make you right,
make you so right that you will never feel that twinge again!
Hey, get your procedure here! Come on, come on now!
Those of you who feel run down, not right, under the weather,
down in the dumps, under the humps, draggin', saggin', laggin',
not up to shaggin', you can be cured, inured, unenterred, preferred,
preserved, protected, and defended! Hey lady, how about that
energy you've had trouble finding? And your son, is he behaving
like he should? We can calm him down and pick you up!
We can make you feel like a new person! You sir, wouldn't you
like to be a new man? And you there, miss? Wouldn't you
like to be the woman you always knew you could be?
We can make you feel just right, air tight, early night,
a must see sight, a delicious bite! But come on, come on now,
you gotta come on and get your procedure here! No waiting,
no waiting, no hesitating! Step right up and get your operation!
Get yourself fixed up, get yourself made whole, get yourself
back to being yourself! Let us take away the pain! You heard
me right! Let us take away the pain! We can put hands on, and
hands in, and caring hands all over, and caring hands to make
your hurting hands do cartwheels! Yes you heard me right, I said
cartwheels! You there, can you still do a cartwheel?
No? Well then you better come on in and get yourself healed!
Come on, come on now! Get your procedure! Step up here!
Don't be the last to get yourself together! Come on,
come on now! Five minutes 'til procedure! Plenty of tables!
Hey, get your procedure! Come on, come on now!

What the President Didn't Say

If we try to send you off
to endless war… don't go. You who
refuse I'm sure would stand shoulder
to shoulder with all of us if
an enemy ever marches down
our streets looking for conquest.
Why go looking for war in other
people's streets and lands? To take
the war to them, to be preemptive,
to be aggressive, you are told. But
why do they always live in huts
and squalor and starve and
look out at us with mournful eyes
and sighs of pain? Can these be those
who threaten us? Why do their warriors
attack with sticks and stones? Are they
who we are protecting freedom from?
Aren't we just plain invading them?
An invasion sounds so much better labeled
as a fight for some kind of freedom
or as our right to defend ourselves.
If we try to send you off to fight these
wars, don't go. Don't listen to us.
Why should you be sent to die
in a land that is not yours, killing
the defenders of that which is not yours,
but belongs to those who were born there?
Would you want them taking and occupying
your land for you? If you were them,
wouldn't you fight you? You are supposed
to believe that going to a country you know
nothing about and killing those
designated to be your enemy, whose
mothers have never mocked you, whose
neighbors and friends have never
cursed you, whose brothers have never

struck you, and yet are still expected by us,
your leaders, to convince
yourself of the right to shoot at
them, because if you don't, they will shoot
you. I suppose a thief breaking into
your home in the middle of the night
could say the same thing, being inside
your house in the dead of night, that he had
every right to shoot you dead because you
were trying to shoot him. It matters whose
house we're in, you know, it matters.
Do you young men and women belong
in a country you don't belong in,
getting shot fighting an enemy
you had to *learn* to hate?
The call to patria nostra is but
a call to your peril from those who would
profit by putting you in harm's way.
Don't listen to them, and if I, yes,
even I, say it, turn a deaf ear. A light heart
is wasted in war. Lives are wasted in war.
Go, be free, live your life, and
never let anyone like me tell you it is
right for you to lose it doing my or
anyone else's bidding. Go now, be free,
live life, it will pass soon enough. Don't
let me or anyone push you from it. Go now
and tell the children and the squirrels,
and let my mother know, she worries so.

Witsa

When I was young,
I knew too little and tried
too hard, and the women
said I was naive,
and drew away.

When I was older,
I learned more and tried
being hard, and the women
said I was too experienced,
and drove away.

When I was middle-aged,
I knew too much and hardly
tried, and the women
said I was not as I seemed,
and flew away.

While now that I'm old,
I again know too little and try
too hard, and the women
say I had my chance,
and float away.

A professional director, producer, actor, writer, teacher, and musician for over fifty years, Dennis Collins Johnson has headed entertainment production companies as executive director and artistic director. He continues to teach improvisation, on-camera acting, voice artistry, stage acting, public speaking, and performance workshops. His most cherished accomplishment is having raised four children as a single father. He can be contacted at dennis@rollickingproductions.com

Made in the USA
Middletown, DE
11 April 2022

63778830R00093